M000313141

FULL CIRCLE

JAMES RAFFERTY

Pacific Press® Publishing Association
Nampa, Idaho
Oshawa, Ontario, Canada

Graphic design by MCM Design Studio, LLC.

Copyright © 2001 by Pacific Press® Publishing Association
All rights reserved
Printed in the United States of America

All Scripture quotations are from the King James Version unless otherwise
noted. NKJV indicates the New King James Version. NIV indicates the New
International Version. NASB indicates the New American Standard Bible.

All emphasis and words in brackets within
quotations are added by the author.

ISBN: 0-8163-1853-0

01 02 03 04 05 • 5 4 3 2 1

Contents

5
A Word of Introduction

8
How It All Started

13
The Mission of Christ—Discovered

21
The Mystery—Illustrated

29
Ambassadors for Christ

37
Conscientious Christians

44
Tag

50
The Beam That Blinds

56
The Pointing Problem

61
Them and Us

67
SONS OF THUNDER

72
HARSH WORDS FROM MARTIN LUTHER

78
I DID IT UZZA'S WAY

83
THE PERFECT CONFLICT

89
FINAL THOUGHTS

A Word of Introduction

As soon as I read the letter on the inside page of the *Review,* my heart ached. Then, perhaps, I'm a little too sensitive. Let me share it with you:

> *I don't attend church anymore. I started back recently and was chided by a member because I left between Sabbath School and the church service.*
> *I have all the hurt I can stand in my personal life. I sure don't need the church inflicting any more hurt.*

Well, what do you think? No big deal, you say? I hope not, because this wounded person represents a large number of former church members in North America. Most of them probably know, and even love, the basic Adventist message, yet their hearts are in conflict with a judgmental spirit that too often rears its ugly head—right on our shoulders!

Of course, there are other letters to the *Review.* Some of them read quite the opposite, expressing fear about falling standards and theological compromise. This produces a different conflict. Perhaps you have witnessed it. Two members of the same church commence to calmly discuss some important yet controversial issue like the nature of Christ. As they continue, voice volumes increase. They begin interrupting each other until finally these "brethren" are red in the face, generating more heat than light. From then on, they are devout enemies and your local church is their battlefield.

Now put these two perspectives together for the big picture, if you dare. What do you see? I see members of a church that claims to be the remnant of Bible prophecy fighting over theological differences while hurting souls are running for our doors—to get out, not in! This scenario illustrates one of the greatest needs in the church today, "the ministry of reconciliation" (see 2 Corinthians 5:19).

This message found a voice at the close of an evangelistic crusade in the Philippines. I admonished members new and old to consider the description of God's remnant church found in Revelation 12:17: "And the dragon was *wroth* with the woman, and went to *make war* with the remnant of her seed"—STOP! "You may find a lot of infighting taking place in the church," I explained. "But don't be discouraged. Satan is enraged at this church. He wants to make you angry at it too. Just keep your eyes on Jesus, no matter what."

Many of us may think there is a new item to add to the list of characteristics of God's remnant church: "Characteristic Number 6: Various groups of angry, fighting people." (If our evangelists choose not to use this point in their Remnant Church sermon, I'll understand.)

You see, I still remember my first six months as a new member. I was sure I had arrived in heaven. I just knew these people must already be sprouting wings. The only problem was how uncomfortable I felt worshiping with all these saints, since I was such a sinner. I would say to myself, "You're here because of Jesus; you're here because of Jesus; don't worry about what people think of you." Being a new convert, just out of the world, I felt people looked down at me. They never did. They rejoiced to see my new faith. But I felt that way, nonetheless. Then, in time, the picture started to clear, shattering my naive image of a perfect church. One of the most devastating revelations was when I discovered that the pastor was still human.

Noticing the failures of others brought an attitude change in me. It was no longer "What a sinner I am." It was "What a sinner everyone else is." Initially I didn't discern the shift. I was just looking for that perfect group of saints—the *"true* church."

At some time or another each one of us has to grapple with the condition of our church. Yet, once we resolve *that* conflict, we may still have to struggle with the strugglers, who, like ourselves, may question the church's identity.

Eventually I pulled away from Adventism. Don't misunderstand. I continued to believe the message and practice the lifestyle; but, in spirit, I was separated from the organized body. By God's grace, my questions have now been reconciled. Now my greatest hope is that the testimony of my journey will help other honest, questioning souls to find reconciliation.

Here is my story and how God led me back home—again.

CHAPTER ONE

How It All Started

It actually arose from deep inside my heart and caught me by surprise. At first I didn't know what was happening to me. In fact, the ugliness was so effectively disguised that I thought it was righteousness. I should have known better; but I guess I was just too young and inexperienced to see clearly. Let me back up to the beginning.

It all began one hot, summer day with a frantic phone call from my mother.

"Jamie," (she named me *James* but calls me *Jamie*; mothers do that sometimes), "your sister has gotten herself caught up in a cult!"

"Caught up in a cult?" I responded with a degree of disbelief. "You mean like the Jim Jones thing?"

"Yes," my mother went on. "In her letters all she talks about is Jesus."

At this point I was a little skeptical. I had just given my heart to the Lord and all I could talk about was Jesus too!

"Are you sure it's a cult, Mom?"

"Of course, I'm sure!" she responded in a tone somewhat irritated by my question. "It's a religious cult. I'm not sure which one exactly, but you must get her out of it! You're her brother and I'm separated from her by an ocean." (My mother lives in London.)

Shortly after this, my sister started sharing her newly found faith with me. It went something like this:

"James, Sunday is the wrong day to go to church. You should be going to church on Saturday."

"Saturday?" I responded. "Who goes to church on Saturday? That's ridiculous." (We had been raised Catholic and I had never heard of anyone going to church on Saturday.)

On another occasion, she said, "James, you shouldn't listen to rock-n-roll music. It's of the devil." This brought the response, "It doesn't matter what kind of music I listen to. (I played the drums and had a set in my living room.) I don't party anymore and I love Jesus."

The clincher came a week or so later.

"James, you shouldn't eat meat," she insisted. "It's not good for you."

Whoa! That was enough for this brother. I decided that there are times when Mother really does know best—perhaps my sister was involved in a cult.

So I began studying with the Seventh-day Adventist Church. My strategy was simple: find out where they were off biblically and get my sister out. I knew it would be the best way to get to the truth of all these strange ideas she had. And it was.

I still remember my first Bible studies. Minutes before the Bible worker was due to arrive, I hurried through some of the lesson, while watching TV. Actually, my two roommates and

I had two TVs, one on top of the other, so we could watch *both* football games every Sunday. We shared a house in Spokane, Washington. This house had developed a reputation among our peers as a "party house." Into this environment stepped a faithful, God-fearing woman (that is, after I had moved the beer cans away from the front door and cleaned up a little). She brought the Word of God and a copy of the *20th Century Bible Course.*

"How did you do with the lesson study this week?" she would inquire in kind, hopeful tones.

"OK," I would respond, feeling somewhat negligent. "But I didn't quite finish."

"That's fine," she would say. "We can cover it together."

I'm not sure exactly how long our studies continued like this, but I definitely remember the change. It all came about as I started to realize that the Bible could be understood. Just the year before, my mother had sent me a Bible, upon my request. It was the *King James Version* and I could hardly understand any of it. So it sat on my bookshelf collecting dust. But now things were different. Going through the Bible study questions, I was always directed to a Scripture verse or two, which gave the answer. I was amazed! In fact, I began to realize that these Adventists believed as they did because they followed the Bible. It was this Bible-based faith that really attracted me to the Church.

I no longer did the studies while watching TV. In fact, I lost interest in watching TV altogether. My roommates eventually moved out, convinced that the *old* me wasn't coming back. Then, one day, as I walked past my drum set, I noticed that it had gathered a good coating of dust.

"Dust," I thought in disgust. "I never let dust gather on my drums." I cleaned them off quickly and opened my cassette collection of rock favorites, looking for something to play along with. I picked out one of my best tapes—Van Halen— and started scanning through the songs. All of a sudden I came to the title, "Running With the Devil." I was instantly repulsed. "I'm not running with the devil!" I exclaimed to myself. And I immediately took my entire collection, over one hundred popular hit tapes, and threw them in the garbage can. Not because I had to, not because my sister or the Church told me to, but because I wanted to. My experience is best described in the following hymn chorus:

Turn your eyes upon Jesus,
Look full in His wonderful face;
And the things of earth will grow strangely dim
In the light of His glory and grace.

Some time later, I was again talking with my mother on the phone—to tell her that I, too, was becoming a Seventh-day Adventist. How that actually happened is a miracle of God when you consider the circumstances. My motive for studying with the Church was wrong. I was trying to get my sister out, not me in. And my mother was sending me all kinds of negative information. Besides this, I was already going to a nondenominational church and attending a youth group at a Pentecostal Church. Dan, whose witness had led me to Christ, and another Pentecostal friend, were warning me at every opportunity not to study with or become a Seventh-day Adventist.

My roommates also worked to get me back, so to speak. They would put alcohol and drugs in my face to tempt me. (Little did they realize that, with the love of God in my heart, these former pastimes were not the least bit tempting.) One of those roommates also pleaded with me to just be my old self again. Due to our friendship, that appeal was probably more pulling than anything. Yet, somehow, through all of this, I stayed on course. What made the difference? As I look back on it all, I now see that, more than ever, it was simply the "wake 'em up, break 'em up," life-changing, rearranging, immovable, unstoppable Word of the all-powerful God of heaven and earth!

"Is not my word like as a fire? saith the Lord; and like a hammer that breaketh the rock in pieces?" (Jeremiah 23:29). It broke my rocky heart, causing me to love the things I once hated and hate the things I once loved. It can do the same for you, too, if you let it.

CHAPTER TWO

The Mission of Christ—Discovered

Jesus became the foundation and love of my life. I had a deep sense that God was guiding me, first out of a formal religion where I said my prayers every night—whether drunk or sober—to a genuine born-again experience, and now to the remnant church of Bible prophecy! I was thankful. I was excited. And I was zealous! I was home!

Yet, added to my excitement and zeal was a great lack of knowledge. Of course, I had some knowledge. I knew the seventh day was the Bible Sabbath and Sunday, the first day, was not. I knew that people who die are "surely dead," not half-dead. I knew the meaning of the beast, the dragon, the trumpets, and the seals. And I knew that history had arrived at the hour of God's judgment.

But listen! While I knew all this and many other related truths, there was something—Someone—that I didn't know as well as I needed to. I didn't see the character of Jesus clearly enough. I didn't understand the weighty significance of His love and His mission. While I thought I really knew something, I was to find that I knew nothing yet as I ought to know (see 1 Corinthians 8:2).

The telltale signs began very early in my experience. When I went to visit my mother, we argued about religion. When talking with my Christian, fellow worker, who had led me to Jesus, we argued about religion. These weren't just little disagreements. They were red-in-the-face, loud, you're-going-to-see-this-my-way, arguments—the kind that threatens to alienate the best of friends. I've come to believe that arguing about religion, especially when two Christians do it, has to be one of the ugliest sights in the world.

After a time, I was arguing with fellow Adventists. Of course, it was much more polite than disputing with other believers. After all, we were fellow members of the remnant. Still, these differences of opinion, that I did not fully comprehend myself, became the banner under which I stood separate from my brethren.

Have you ever been misdirected while thinking you were on the right road? Being involved in gospel ministry, my family travels more than the average family does. Every once in a great while, when we go for a seminar, I forget to bring a map. Like most males who *think* they have a keen sense of direction, I assure my wife that we will have little problem finding our way because we have the "Drive-Until-You-Find-It plan," also known as DUYFI. It is the second-best thing to having directions, though my wife might describe it as the second-worst thing to being hopelessly lost. What I do is drive . . . and drive . . . and drive . . . and, well, drive some more. Only after exhausting every possible option am I finally convinced that we're lost and need to ask for help. (Male ego has a hard time here.)

The DUYFI method illustrates the spiritual experience that I fell into at this point. When I saw tares in God's church, I forgot the road map and set out to find the perfect remnant people. Friends and spiritual guardians in the church begged me to forsake the search. They had seen numerous groups of people fall into the same trap. But, mistaking zeal for wisdom, I ignored their entreaties, assuring fellow members that I knew where I was going. I even convinced a few others that our destination must be just around the next corner. It never was.

This was a time of endless controversy, not that controversy is wrong in and of itself. The danger is in getting so caught up in it that we are diverted from following Christ.

It is easy to be on a busy freeway and get so caught up in the traffic that you miss your turn. Sometimes the traffic refuses to let us out. That's how it can be with controversy. It can so consume us that we can neither see nor take the right exit. Then we find ourselves on the wrong road directed by the surrounding vehicles.

Though controversy may always surround us, it should never consume us. It is when we are swallowed up by issues that we lose sight of the mission of Christ, the one truth which the Bible says is "without controversy" (1 Timothy 3:16).

Consider Paul's thought in its entirety. "And *without controversy* great is the mystery of godliness: God was manifest in the flesh, justified in the Spirit, seen of angels, preached unto the Gentiles, believed on in the world, received up into glory" (1 Timothy 3:16).

Did you catch it? It's not all that profound and nebulous, which you might expect of a mystery, or is it? The great mystery of our faith is beyond doubt and without question.

God loved us so much that even though He absolutely abhorred everything we represent (sin):

- He came to live with sinners;
- He wrought out righteousness among sinners;
- He tasted death for sinners;
- And He now spends all of His time working in behalf of sinners.

Here is the bottom line: God hates sin, but He loves sinners. Following this theme through the Bible promises to take us right out of controversy, out of freeway traffic and on to our destination. The mission of Christ was not to debate, argue, or judge. He came to save sinners! (See Luke 5:32.)

The apostle Paul calls the mission of Christ for sinners a mystery, though at first glance it almost appears to be a contradiction. A pure and holy God, who hates sin, comes to live and die for wretched, unholy sinners. That's what makes it a mystery, not just to us, but also to the unfallen universe.

"And to make all see what is the *fellowship of the mystery,* which from the beginning of the ages has been hidden in God who created all things through Jesus Christ; to the intent that now the manifold wisdom of God might be made known by the church to the *principalities and powers in the heavenly places,* according to the eternal purpose which He accomplished in Christ Jesus our Lord" (Ephesians 3:9-11, NKJV).

They [unfallen angels] desire to know how Christ could live and work in a fallen world, how He could *mingle with sinful humanity*. It was a *mystery* to them that He who hated sin with intense hatred felt the most tender, compassionate sympathy for the beings that committed sin.

Now comes the challenging part. Are you ready? Ephesians 3 calls us to "make all men see" or "to make plain to everyone" (NIV) "what is the *fellowship* of the mystery...to the intent that now unto the principalities and powers in heavenly places might be known *by the church* the manifold wisdom of God" (Ephesians 3:9, 10). This mysterious love is to be made manifest to men and angels through the church (see Ephesians 3:12-21).

Obedience to the law ("here are they that keep the commandments of God") gives us our identity, while loving those who do not keep the commandments ("love is the fulfilling of the law") gives our identity its substance (see Revelation 12:17; 14:12; Romans 13:10; Galatians 5:14). When we embrace *this* mission, the problems of the remnant become a training ground. Rather than being excuses to leave, problems become opportunities to love as Christ loves, to participate in the mystery of godliness (see Colossians 1:25, 26; Revelation 10:7).

At this point some sincere brother or sister may be thinking, "Love, love, love! That's all we hear about anymore! What about standards? What about the law? What about obedience? What about hating sin?"

Hate for sin is essential (see Genesis 3:15).

Love for sinners is vital (see 1 Corinthians 13).

Here is the goal: kindness, compassion, and sympathy for

the sinner *while* hating sin with a perfect hatred. This was the mystery, the secret passion of the life of Christ.

It's beautiful.

It's desirable.

And it's difficult.

The difficulty is in the love and hate mixture. Because they are opposites, getting them together can be hard. Consider these simple illustrations:

Example 1: We allow love into our hearts for Joe Sinner, but we leave hate for Joe's sin out in the cold.

Example 2: We allow hate into our hearts for Joe's sin, but fail to let love inside our hearts for Joe.

It is here that each of us comes face-to-face with an underlying cause of division in our church. We encounter a church problem, for instance, a couple going through a divorce. Let's say both partners are members. The church is split. Part of the church wants to stress love and sympathy, while the other part seeks to emphasize the standard of justice and hatred for sin. Confusion ensues. Groups are formed. Rumors are flying. Labels stick like velcro. The pastor is caught in the middle. The church board becomes dysfunctional.

Far-fetched?

Wake-up time!

The remedy for these kinds of church differences is the same for each faction—balance. Too simple? A battery has two sides, positive and negative. While these are opposites, both are vital. Try starting your car with only one battery post connected. Get the point?

We need balance—blending together the opposing principles of love and hate. Failure to unite love for the sinner with hate for sin produces two soul-destroying extremes: laxness in dealing with sin on the one hand, or harsh judgment and groundless suspicion on the other.

But what is balance and how do we achieve it?

Colossians 4:6 speaks of the balance of grace (mercy) and salt (justice) when it comes to sharing truth. "Let your speech *always be with grace,* seasoned with *salt,* that you may know *how* you ought to answer each one" (NKJV). Notice that Paul uses salt to illustrate a sprinkling of justice added to a constant helping of grace. Sometimes we get it turned around, emphasizing the salt of God's justice interspersed with a dash of grace. Imagine sitting down to a meal of a large scoop of salt, sprinkled with a few potatoes and wolfing it down. Yuck! In a world that is bland of morality and teeming with apostasy, we can tend to be a little heavy on the salt of justice. Abounding iniquity, making love's grace grow cold, is one of the signs of Christ's second coming (see Matthew 24:12).

At the same time, preaching love, love, love with no justice is like eating potatoes with absolutely no salt or seasoning at all. Blah! This is the opposite extreme—emphasizing God's grace and leaving out the seasoning of pointed truth altogether. When the apostle Paul stressed, "the love of Christ constraineth us," he had just mentioned that "knowing therefore the terror of the Lord, we persuade men" (see 2 Corinthians 5:14, 11).

While in my critical, separatist attitude toward the church, I emphasized justice and obedience to the law. I felt that the church was focusing too much on love, mercy, and grace. These two essential elements are often polarized by sincere, well-meaning, Spirit-led people. Each aspect is necessary for the body of Christ. Our problem is that, while opposites often attract, we tend to repel each other and discord prevails.

Our only safety is to focus entirely upon Jesus, to listen to His voice saying, "This is the way, walk ye in it, when ye turn to the right hand [extreme justice], and when ye turn to the left [extreme mercy]" (Isaiah 30:21, words in brackets added).

In time I discovered the mission of Christ—not just the sacrifice of Christ or the perfect life of Christ—but His mission.

"For the Son of man is come to seek and to save that which was lost" (Luke 19:10).

Then it hit me . . . hard!

I had been looking for the obedient; He was looking for the disobedient. I was on a quest to find the *true* commandment keepers and He came to pursue true commandment breakers. I was searching for the saved; He was searching for the lost.

It was here that my discovery of truth really began—not just intellectual truth (facts and information) but the truth as it is in Jesus (see Ephesians 4:21).

CHAPTER THREE

The Mystery—Illustrated

There he was again, waiting in the driveway. "Doesn't he ever give up?" I remember thinking. "He" being Elder Stan Folkenberg. Though he is now resting until Jesus comes, at the time he was a semiretired stewardship director of our local conference. He was also our shadow, or so it seemed to us. "Us" consisted of Ty Gibson and myself, then working together in a newly formed, independent ministry that had pulled away from the organized church. And Stan, well, he just didn't believe that these two, fairly new converts were seeing the whole picture. So there he was in the driveway, again, with some new study or statement to share with us from Inspiration.

This was a time when many of our fellow church members would hardly speak to us at all. And you couldn't blame them. When you are seen as tearing down something people have dedicated their lives to building up, they tend to take it personally. Yet it seemed that Stan always had something to say. Sometimes he would go out of his way to say it. Like the time we were making some shelves for our new bookstore (at a church member's house). All of a sudden, there was Stan. He had popped in with the latest quote that he was sure would help us sort it all out. Or occasionally he just pulled us aside for a few minutes while we were buying books at the local ABC. But the most memorable of all his efforts were those occasions when he just sat in the driveway waiting for us, like a longing father patiently waiting for his wayward sons.

While he ever opposed our position of separation from the body, Stan kept the torch of love burning in his heart. Stan never saw us come back to God's church, but we'll fill him in after resurrection morn.

When you think about it, all of us were on Someone else's heart when it broke 2,000 years ago. We have all pulled away from Christ in one way or another, but Jesus has refused to give up on us (see 2 Peter 3:9). And because Christ takes every opportunity to search us out and talk to us through His Spirit, we can find reconciliation today. The very foundation of this hope lies in our Savior's ability to manifest love and compassion to both the wayward sinner as well as the self-righteous *separatist* (Greek for "Pharisee"). This tremendous attribute so necessary for drawing others to Him is illustrated in two of the most remarkable stories found in the Gospels.

The first is probably the most unusual trial ever decided. You would never have predicted or even chanced to guess at such an outcome. The final verdict contradicted all the evidence and eyewitness reports. In fact, the prosecution eventually withdrew from the case and even the accused was astonished by the final decision.

It is the true incident of a woman caught in flagrant commission of a crime punishable by death. Her criminal activity was adultery. Having been caught in the very act, she would be an easy scapegoat to entrap Christ, or so the Pharisees had reasoned. And their plan seemed to be working as they hauled the shameful wretch into His presence. But the tables would be turned on these self-righteous hypocrites by the world's best Defense Lawyer (see 1 John 2:1).

As He assessed the situation, it was easy for Jesus to see with His own eyes that this woman was guilty. Christ also heard with His own ears the condemnation placed upon her by the Pharisees. But what a startling shock it must have been to those sanctimonious religionists when He stooped down to scribble their own, individual, secret sins in the dust. How strangely unwilling they suddenly became to respond to the challenge, "He that is without sin among you, let him first cast a stone at her" (John 8:7).

Then, in tones of the deepest compassion, Jesus spoke to the trembling, blameworthy woman bowed before Him. "Woman, where are those thine accusers? Hath no man condemned thee? She said, No man, Lord. And Jesus said unto her, Neither do I condemn thee: go, and sin no more" (John 8:10, 11). Amazing grace, how sweet the sound!

God incarnate came face-to-face with guilty, fallen humanity and offered mercy, acceptance, and forgiveness. This was the mystery of His mission—illustrated.

A prophecy written hundreds of years before Christ was born describes the mystery in this way:

> *And there shall come forth a rod out of the stem of Jesse, and a Branch shall grow out of his roots: And the spirit of the Lord shall rest upon him, the spirit of*

wisdom and understanding, the spirit of counsel and
might, the spirit of knowledge and of the fear of the
Lord; And shall make him of quick understanding in
the fear of the Lord: and he shall not judge after the
sight of his eyes, neither reprove after the hearing of his
ears (Isaiah 11:1-3).

You've got to admit that it's pretty mysterious not to judge or reprove people according to what you see and hear. It definitely comes as a challenge to all of us in church relationships today.

As this truth began to unfold before me, I realized that I had failed to follow the method of Christ in dealing with accusations against another woman, the Bride of Christ. Our Savior's merciful treatment of a guilty, culpable woman revealed some important principles to my mind concerning my unmerciful treatment of God's remnant church:

1) I, too, should have been hesitant to judge the church by outward appearance. Though this can be difficult, Christ admonishes us to be cautious in this area, in case we pull up wheat with tares (see Matthew 13:28-30).

2) Christ was influenced by the Spirit of God, not the accusations of men, which led Him to work for restoration rather than condemnation of the erring (see Galatians 6:1).

3) And finally, those who are forward in accusing others are usually just as guilty. This is a simple fact of human nature. We judge, but we do the same things (see Romans

2:1-3). I am personally learning to let the inc' judge others be a red flag that all may not be in oru. my own life (see Matthew 7:1-5).

While God's church has not been what it should be, Christ works to save, Phariseeism to destroy. Before Christ said to the woman, "go and sin no more," He revealed His undying mercy and forgiveness. But here's the point. Holding back condemnation and mingling love and acceptance with faithful admonition make Christ's words a renewing power in our lives rather than a burden on our backs (see 1 John 5:3). This is the balance of grace and truth, of mercy and justice: unabashed, shameless love for the transgressor while maintaining a standard against sin.

No, it is not enough to simply know what is wrong and condemn it. People need renewal. Sinners need hope. The church needs empowerment!

Jesus did not condone this woman's sin, nor does He condone the sins of His church today. He simply treated her in such a manner that she could receive the words "go and sin no more" (John 8:11). Yet Christ's actions were a direct, undeniable rebuke to the way in which the Pharisees dealt with the erring. In using this woman as a pawn to entrap Christ, they displayed greater concern for upholding the law than for saving sinners. "Confident of their own righteousness" their obedience to the law had become their savior and they "looked down on everybody else" (Luke 18:9, NIV).

Which brings us to the second illustration of the mystery of Godliness exemplified by our Savior. It is only four verses in length. The punch line is all of five words. Nevertheless, it gives us a most profound insight into love and hate.

Tribute collectors confronted Simon Peter, one of Christ's disciples. Their purpose, unbeknownst to Peter, was to ensnare Christ:

"When they had come to Capernaum, those who received the temple tax came to Peter, and said, 'Does your Teacher not pay the temple tax?' " (Matthew 17:24, NKJV).

Always quick to speak, especially in defense of his Master, Peter responded with an undiscerning "Yes." (verse 25, NKJV). Of course, my Master will pay this tax. "After all," he must have reasoned, "it is required in the writings of Moses" (see Exodus 30:13).

Poor Peter. Little did he realize the craftiness of those two schemers. Sure, they wanted Christ to refuse payment of the temple tax. Then, accusing Him of holding the Law of Moses in disrepute, they could impede His ministry. They were still delighted, however, with Peter's rash willingness to pay the tax. Everyone knew that prophets were exempt from this tax. So why would Christ pay it if He were, not only a prophet, but the Messiah of Israel, Himself?

Jesus, however, understood their true aim. While they waited outside, smiling with diabolical delight that their trap was working so well, Christ straightened out Peter on the issue.

"And when he had come into the house, Jesus anticipated him, saying, 'What do you think, Simon? From whom do the kings of the earth take customs or taxes, from their sons or from strangers?'

"Peter said to Him, 'From strangers.'

"Jesus said to him, 'Then the sons are free'" (Matthew 17:25, 26, NKJV).

In other words, Christ was not obligated to pay this temple tax. But now what? Impetuous Peter had already given his word. Would bearing false witness be added to the accusation of disregarding the temple rites?

Before Peter could say a word, Christ did something remarkable. Rather than justify Himself before those who were trying to entrap Him, He said, " *'Nevertheless, lest we offend them . . .'* " (Matthew 17:27, NKJV).

Pause on that thought for a moment. Lest He offend whom? Two men who are trying to entrap Him, who probably don't care whether He lives or dies? Surely Christ was more concerned about His own reputation than offending these two deceivers and the religious defamation league that sent them. Guess again!

This is where we catch an awesome glimpse of the battle between love and hate. In the life of Christ, love conquered hate every time. Jesus was not willing to offend even those who hated Him if He could help it. That's my Savior! And yours!

Christ continued: " 'Go to the sea, cast in a hook, and take the fish that comes up first. And when you have opened its mouth, you will find a piece of money; take that, and give it to them for Me and you' " (Matthew 17:27, NKJV).

I can picture the tribute collectors returning to the temple with their report. In excitement the religious leaders learn that Jesus has paid the tax. Then—much to their dismay—they realize that their trap has misfired. A "small" miracle accompanies any use of this defaming evidence, a miracle significant enough to substantiate, rather than dilute, the people's confidence in Christ.

This story touches on an essential element, a key ingredient as to how Christ worked to reach the hearts of sinners. He was filled with the divine love of God, a love that made little distinction between friend and foe. Unlike our natural response to those who oppose us, Jesus Christ longed to reach the priests and teachers and, as this story represents, He left no means untried.

These two stories illustrate the way Jesus Christ related to the unrighteous and the self-righteous. The Pharisees claimed to be defenders of the truth, while lacking proper judgment, love, mercy, and faith (see Matthew 23:23; Luke 11:42). This deficiency was made apparent in their attitude toward the woman caught in adultery, as seen in the first story. While Jesus defended her with compassion and forgiveness, they treated her as a hopeless case worthy only of condemnation. Still Christ loved the self-righteous priests, as evidenced in the second story, even as He loved the erring woman. And He loved me, as a sinner in the world, and as a self-righteous opponent of His church.

I began reevaluating my attitude. In time, I began a focused study on this Bible verse (Galatians 6:1): "Brethren," Paul exhorts, "if a man be overtaken in a fault, ye which are spiritual, restore such an one in the spirit of meekness; considering thyself, lest thou also be tempted."

In this Bible verse I sensed a meaning that had been hidden from my understanding, but which promised, upon discovery, to challenge my separatist stance. I pondered the thought, "ye that are spiritual." Before long I found myself thinking that perhaps being spiritual equates to more than doing everything right outwardly. Maybe it points to the attitude, the spirit, and the heart. Indeed, it does, as I was about to find out.

CHAPTER FOUR

Ambassadors for Christ

L et me take you back momentarily to my conversion story. It was another Friday night and the house was full of the usual bustle stirred up by three young roommates at the start of a weekend. There was plenty of alcohol, drugs, friends, and loud music, but tonight it didn't hold the usual appeal for me. Something was missing. What that something was, I understood about as well as I understand Latin, which made it all the worse. All I knew was that I sensed an emptiness that nothing around me was filling.

The following night I felt the same way, but it was stronger. The feelings of despair drove me to my room, away from what now seemed to be senseless party life. Then Dan's words came to my mind. Dan was a fellow worker. We used to party together, that is, until he became a Christian. Now all we did together was talk about Jesus. (That is, *he* talked about Jesus, not me!) In our last encounter, he had explained to me how I could ask Christ to forgive my sins and to be my personal Savior. I had not felt the least bit interested at the time; I was actually more irritated than anything else. Yet now, his simple words pressed home to my vacant heart as if they were the only answer for the present nothingness I felt inside. I went to my knees at the bottom of my bed. I repeated his words as best I could remember them and added some of my own:

"Dear God, You said that You can forgive me of my sins and cleanse my life so it can be just as if I had never sinned. I know I can't do it myself. You know my weaknesses and how I've tried to be good and always fail. If You want me to be a Christian, You're going to have to take these things away from me because I can't. I accept You into my heart now, as my Savior, and I believe that You have forgiven me. In Jesus' name, amen."

That was it. No peals of thunder or electric emotions jolting my body to the floor. Just a simple prayer coupled with a sense that God would be true to His word. And He was. From that moment on, my old life was undesirable. What made it so? I believe it was the sense of God's forgiving love so freely poured out upon me. The fact that He had forgiven me filled the vacuum in my heart, and became a constraining power in my life.

As I look back on my conversion experience, I now see a valuable lesson. It has to do with our methods of reaching people for Christ and with what that Bible verse we read a little while ago means when it says, "Brethren, if a man be overtaken in a fault, ye which are spiritual, restore such an one in the spirit of meekness; considering thyself, lest thou also be tempted" (Galatians 6:1).

You see, over the years I've met various types of people and have seen all kinds of methods designed to bring revival to the church. Consider the man who stood out in front of churches dressed in a white robe and sandals, with a trumpet hanging from his shoulder, and carrying a shepherd's staff. He held up signs calling the church *Babylon,* which means "confusion," though in conversation he seemed a little confused himself.

There were others who engaged me in diverse, meaningful conversation about the intricate details of the finer points concerning complex, difficult-to-grasp, essential-for-salvation theories, which must be carefully analyzed for many years to understand in a simple manner, though explaining them to others might never be an option because by that time it will be too late so—REPENT! Did you get all that? I never did.

And then there was the sincere brother who used a megaphone each Sabbath to blare out assorted accusations at arriving members until he was confronted or arrested, after which he would descend upon another church. (He had lots of persecution stories to tell.)

There was even a fellow who just knew, based on past mistakes that all the church leaders were up to no good. That's why he had personally spent thousands of dollars on private investigators to secretly follow the movements of various leaders in the church. His stated purpose was to catch them in the act of some horrendous sin so that he could expose them for the wicked apostates they really were.

Are we to conclude that these are examples of what Paul meant when he said "ye which are spiritual" are to deal with the erring? (See Galatians 6:1.) Does being spiritual mean spending thousands of dollars investigating the possible sins of others rather than *wasting* it on missionary endeavors like building churches, preaching the gospel, and feeding the hungry? After all, how can we deal with the faulty if we do not first dig up all their faults, right? Wrong!

As Christians each one of us has been given a special ministry. That is, every person in Christ, every "new creature," no matter what our talents or position, has been entrusted with an individual work to do for others. It is the "ministry of reconciliation," as stated in 2 Corinthians 5:17-19.

Reconciliation simply means "restoration" or "to restore." It points to the most important information available to the world today—reclamation. Satan legally claimed the human race through Adam's disobedience; but at the Cross we were reclaimed by God through Christ (see Hebrews 2:9). What a glorious truth! Think about it—the legal prey of the devil set free by the love of the God we have resisted and defied (see Romans 5:6). Individually accepting what has been done for us in Christ propels our lives into a ministry of reconciliation for those about us (see 2 Corinthians 5:19, 20).

But how are we to bring sinners to repentance and the worldly-minded back to the straight and narrow? Is it by accosting them with megaphones while dressed up as latter-day prophets, or spending thousands of dollars to hire investigators to search out their sins so that we can expose them?

Paul is clear: "God was in Christ, reconciling the world unto Himself, *not imputing their trespasses unto them;* and hath committed unto us the word of reconciliation" (2 Corinthians 5:19). Another translation makes it clearer yet—"God was reconciling the world to Himself in Christ, *not counting men's sins against them.* And He has committed to us the message of reconciliation" (NIV). In the words of the psalmist, "He hath not dealt with us after our sins; nor rewarded us according to our iniquities" (Psalms 103:10).

And in the words of Peter, "For Christ also hath once suffered for sins, the just for the unjust, *that* He might *bring us* to God, being put to death in the flesh, but quickened by the Spirit" (1 Peter 3:18).

No, God is not playing make-believe. He is fully aware of our every sin. If anyone has an accurate list of the failures of His people, He does (see Ezekiel 8). But our Creator understands how to draw a sinner to the path of repentance. And it is not through judging and condemnation, but through love—"the goodness of God leadeth thee to repentance" (Romans 2:4; see also John 3:16, 17; Titus 3:3, 4).

At sin's inception, God had one of two choices:

1) Treat us as we deserve—guilty—and wipe mankind off the face of the earth; or
2) Treat us as we don't deserve—innocent—and save us from immediate death and give us life.

The fact that you are reading these words right now is positive proof that He did not pursue the first choice.

In Genesis 2:17 we read, "But of the tree of the knowledge of good and evil, thou shalt not eat of it: for *in the day* that thou eatest thereof thou shalt surely die." Why didn't we die? Because as soon as there was sin, there was a Savior, "the Lamb slain from the foundation of the world" (Revelation 13:8). This is the mystery of Christ's mission—initiated.

We are not, in actuality, innocent. Neither is God pretending that we are innocent. We are guilty. From the common criminal to the present pope, "all have sinned and come short of the glory of God" (Romans 3:23).

In stark reality, we should be dead, "for the wages of sin is death" (Romans 6:23). We are not dead for one reason: Jesus Christ is "the Savior of *all men,* specially of those that believe" (1 Timothy 4:10).

"And He is the propitiation for our sins: and *not for ours only,* but also for the sins of the whole world" (1 John 2:2).

"For there is one God, and one mediator between God and men, the man Christ Jesus. Who gave Himself a ransom *for all,* to be testified in due time" (1 Timothy 2:5, 6).

By God's boundless mercy, all have been saved from the immediate consequences of sin.

Driving to a friend's house on my Kawasaki 550 LTD, I experienced firsthand being alive when I should have been dead. It was a cool summer evening so I put on my leather jacket and helmet. Cruising up a two-lane street toward a red light, I noticed an oncoming car waiting to turn. About halfway up the last block before the intersection, the light turned green. I sped up quickly, along with the car in the lane next to me. We were at a fairly high speed when the car waiting to turn began to pull across the intersection. Then the driver of that car decided he couldn't clear the intersection before we got there, so he stopped suddenly—in my lane!

From that point on, everything was slow motion. A flood of thoughts came to my mind. "This is it! I guess I am going to die in a motorcycle accident after all. God, help me." After the initial crash, I went airborne.

"Tuck and roll, tuck and roll," I thought. Bump, bump, bump, bump, bump, went my helmet on the hard pavement as my body rolled violently across the asphalt.

Working in a hospital, I had seen numerous motorcycle accidents, most with devastating consequences. I lay motionless, but conscious, hesitant to move. I was sent to emergency for a checkup and X-rays. My motorcycle was completely totaled, but nothing showed up on me except a few bruises and an overwhelming certainty that God had saved my life.

Paul recognized this saving attitude of God toward sinners as a power to draw us away from sin. "For the love of Christ constraineth us; because we thus judge, that if One died for all, then were all dead. And that He died for all, that they which live should not henceforth live unto themselves, but unto Him which died for them, and rose again" (2 Corinthians 5:14, 15).

Sin brought a legal mandate of death upon all of us. Yet in His infinite mercy, God made Christ "to be sin for us, who knew no sin; that," (and this is the potential of every human being) "we might be made the righteousness of God in Him" (2 Corinthians 5:21).

The entire human race justly deserves death but God "giveth to all life, and breath, and all things; . . . That, [so that, in order that] they should seek the Lord, if haply they might feel after Him, and find Him, though He be not far from every one of us: for *in Him* we live, and move, and have our being" (Acts 17:25, 27-28).

From sin's insidious inception, God put the whole world "in Him," Jesus Christ. By bestowing mercy on Adam and Eve, rather than judgment, God has given them and us, their offspring, everything we don't deserve. This truth, more fully understood, holds the power of repentance for every sinner.

Yes, there is a variety of approaches we can take to try to bring people to repentance. But there is one way that stands above them all. God has given us this method by example and precept. He offers it to us; we have only to accept. And our acceptance declares us to be "ambassadors for Christ," the highest ranking official from one government to another (see 2 Corinthians 5:20).

Do our present methods of dealing with sinners represent the government of heaven? In our manner toward the faults of our fellow travelers, do they see the principles outlined in God's Word at work in us? In my life, they hadn't.

I was separating from the church because of the sins of its members, rather than ministering to the body in spite of those sins. If God's attitude had been like mine, we would be dead. The contrast between our attitude and God's is obvious. God loves us with an everlasting love while we love each other with an everlasting question mark.

I treated the church according to its actual condition rather than its potential. In fact, the church could never measure up as far as I was concerned. Even when it did good, I looked for the bad. (It's the old "the glass is half empty rather than half full" perspective.)

I finally concluded that the church could do no good. "Can any good thing come out of the church?" was my perpetual question. I treated rumors as facts, and facts as unpardonable sins. What led me to develop such an attitude? Since you're wondering, let me tell you.

CHAPTER FIVE

Conscientious Christians

When I look back and try to analyze what caused me to pull away from God's church, I now see that there were a number of factors. One of the most influential was listening to reports on the failings of the church. There were Barnhouse and Martin, Davenport, and the medal to the pope, to name a few. These were followed by our doctrinal changes in 1980, the nature of Christ controversy, new theology, and trademark lawsuits, to name some more.

As I was initially introduced to the faults of the church, I was given a neat, three-ringed binder containing full documentation in sequential order. (It's probably still on file somewhere.) But the most significant point that I can remember, the one factor that influenced me more than any other, was where these reports were coming from. The people sharing this information seemed to be conscientious brethren living up to the light God had laid out for His church. While my high expectations of God's remnant were being deflated, here were people who seemed to be all that I had envisioned. It was the impact of their outward piety that tipped the scale.

I began to side against the church and finally, I put my entire confidence in whatever report came from the "conscientious brethren," deciding that they were living up to the light and could, therefore, be trusted.

In time, I started to realize that I was making a big mistake. One principle alone, "cease ye from man," should have been enough (see Isaiah 2:22). But the influence of people who manifest strict outward obedience to truth can wield a powerful hold on those who want to do what's right. Of course, this is not a new problem. Neither is the power of influence of outward conscientiousness. After all, it was this very same power wielded by the very same type of people that led to ultimate rejection of a nation's King. And the religious leaders of Christ's time were definitely conscientious; at least it seemed that way. They prayed long prayers, paid a faithful tithe, and were known for always citing Scripture. Even Christ commended them as men whose words should be followed. The only problem was, they didn't *really* walk the walk. "Yes," said Christ, "do as they *say,* just don't do as they do" (see Matthew 23:2, 3).

This was because while the Pharisees put a great deal of effort into the observance of details, they overlooked the "weightier" themes of faith, mercy, and the love of God (see Matthew 23:23; Luke 11:42). Yet because the Pharisees were outwardly righteous, the people were deceived (see Matthew 23:25-28) and followed their every word. What's more, the populous believed whatever report came from the lips of these professed defenders of the faith.

How shrewd, how clever, how utterly tragic—defenders of truth who failed to practice that truth in their own hearts.

Outward obedience, inward iniquity. Laden with intellect, void of reality. A form of godliness, a heart of stone.

The Pharisees were self-deceived—perfect Laodiceans—unconscious of their own need (see Revelation 3:17). While believing themselves to be the sole guardians of the truth, in actuality they were truth's worst enemies. They tracked Christ with a passion, searching endlessly for every loophole by which to condemn Him. Then one day their opportunity appeared. "And it came to pass, as Jesus sat at meat in the house, behold, many publicans and sinners came and sat down with him and his disciples" (Matthew 9:10).

That was it! Now they had eyewitness reports. If Jesus was God-sent, why, as it had been rumored, did He hang out with the wrong crowd? And if He was genuinely pious, why were these unconverted, worldly publicans and outcasts drawn to Him? Wouldn't true religion be boring and unattractive to them? It was time to put forth their complaint—*to the disciples.*

The Pharisees were not just watching for mistakes in the life of Christ; they also scrutinized His followers. It wasn't long before they found something they could construe as blatant apostasy.

"At that time Jesus went on the sabbath day through the corn; and his disciples were an hungered, and began to pluck the ears of corn, and to eat" (Matthew 12:1).

Sure enough. Now they had the evidence they needed to accuse Christ's disciples. "His disciples desecrate the Sabbath! How can their ministry be of God!" they must have exclaimed to each other. And they went forth to make their complaint—*to Jesus.*

Please notice. It is the *method* of their inquiry, the *way* they go about making their complaints, that reveals the utter delusion of their concern. They complain *about* those in error rather than *to* them.

There is nothing new under the sun (see Ecclesiastes 1:9). When accusations cause doubt and dissension, when complaints are noised abroad *about* others but not *to* them, we are repeating the spirit of Phariseeism.

The true motive of Christ's detractors becomes clear. They were seeking to disrupt Christ's ministry by causing division within and withdrawing support from without. They did this by disguising finger-pointing and accusing under the veil of *faithful* reproof.

Jesus lovingly, but firmly, rebuked their manner of dealing with the erring. He taught that it was the faulty, the sinners and the outcasts of society who would accept the gospel of His grace.

One of the greatest violations in need of the Savior's correction was their failure to follow gospel order. Disregard of this principle revealed the true colors of these apparently religious people. And it will test our own integrity too. Even many who *appear to be conscientious Christians* are hindered by pride and self-esteem from going privately to those whom they think in error, that they may talk with them in the Spirit of Christ and pray together for one another.

This was definitely a test of my integrity. Like the conscientious Pharisees, I, too, had been violating gospel order when it came to church problems. What a challenge it was not to have our local pastor for lunch—as in criticizing his message, not in feeding him food. Then came an eventful sermon on church authority. My fellow workers were up in arms, anxious to vacate the pews and begin a meeting to find fault with the sermon. But I determined not to attend because, on my way out, the pastor had kindly requested my input on his presentation. This was an opportunity to practice gospel order (see Matthew 18:15-17). Later that week, after prayer and study, I shared with the pastor my concern:

"I agree with much of what you said," I explained, "but this is where I disagree and here's why."

His response took me completely off guard. "You're right," he humbly replied. "What should I do?"

"Well," my head was spinning—I had no idea what to say, "let the Lord lead you," I sheepishly sidestepped.

The next Sabbath this pastor apologized from the pulpit for the very point that I had brought to his attention.

This experience marked a turning point in my attitude toward the church. In one short sentence, this pastor had done what the arguments of numerous pastors and conference men had always failed to do. And I'm sure he didn't even realize it. In that brief exchange I learned to give our church leaders the benefit of the doubt. It was a powerful lesson I hope never to forget.

Yes, reproving wrong is part of our duty as Christians, "but it is to the wrongdoer himself that we are to present the wrong. We are not to make it a matter of comment and criticism among ourselves; nor even after it is told to the church, are we at liberty to repeat it to others. A knowledge of the faults of Christians will be only a cause of stumbling to the unbelieving world; and by dwelling upon these things, we ourselves can receive only harm; for it is by beholding that we become changed. While we seek to correct the errors of a brother, the Spirit of Christ will lead us to shield him, as far as possible, from the criticism of even his own brethren" and more importantly "from the censure of the unbelieving world" (*The Desire of Ages,* p. 441).

Now I had learned firsthand the difference between just plain reproving and giving *faithful* reproof. If done faithfully, reproof will be carried out in harmony with God's provisions for correcting the erring. For example, the purpose of reproof should be to "restore" those who are in error and sin, not to gossip about them (see Galatians 6:1).

If we talk about the weaknesses of the church, especially if we broadcast them for all to hear via newsletter, tape, or video, we give Satan opportunity to triumph by exposing our weaknesses to our enemies. Christ did *not* say, "When the sins and failures of the church have been preached in all the world, then shall the end come." Our message to the world by pen and voice is the "good news" of the gospel, not the bad news of the church (see Matthew 24:14).

In fact, there can be a tremendous outgrowth in using the following approach: When you think your brother is pursuing a wrong course, go to him and invite him to compare notes with you. Ask him if he is sure of his conclusions.

Here is the problem. We take up negative reports concerning others; we listen to and believe them without finding out *firsthand* whether or not they are true.

For example, not long ago I received a call, "Brother So-and-So is teaching such-and-such."

"So-and-So is teaching such-and-such?" I asked carefully. "Are you sure?"

"Yes," was the response, "and it's deadly heresy."

"Well, how do you know that So-and-So is teaching such-and-such?" I inquired further. "Have you listened to his tapes or read his material?"

"Well, not exactly. Just tidbits here and there. But I've heard. . . ."

"Yes," I replied, "but it is easy to be misrepresented. It has happened to me often. Even the Bible writers have been misquoted and misinterpreted. Why don't you call or write So-and-So?"

"Oh, that wouldn't really be any use. I'm sure he would never listen to me. Besides, we'd probably just go around in circles."

Consider yourself as a conscientious Christian. How would you feel if people were talking about you without giving you the benefit of the doubt by asking for clarification? What would you do if all your mistakes were broadcast for the world to read?

The warning I would like to sound here is not much different from what Jesus had in mind when His stern rebukes fell upon the Pharisees (see Matthew 23). He cautioned the people not to allow outwardly conscientious religionists to be the deciding factor against the truth, namely, Himself. Especially if these religionists were heavy on the standards, such as tithe, and light on the principles, such as mercy, faith, and love. Is this an appropriate warning for us today? Keep reading.

CHAPTER SIX

Tag

"Tag—you're it!"

Most of us remember this innocent childhood game. You run down a certain person, usually someone you think you can catch, and tag them. Then he's "it" and he has to run down someone else. As adults some of us still play tag, but in a different way. We run down people and tag them with our words. The adult version is called Talebearing And Gossip—TAG.

It is a sad fact that the faults of others and negative news are what people want to hear. In this respect we sometimes "heap" to ourselves "teachers" who will report on the church's failures because we have "itching ears" anxious to hear the latest wrongdoing (see 2 Timothy 4:3). The problem lies in fallen human nature which thrives on the negative emphasis. As illustrated by our media system today, the more negative the news, the more people seem to take an interest.

Many of us actually consider it a virtue to expose the wrongs of others. When we started our ministry, the popular opinion of those surrounding us was that giving publicity to the errors and misdoings of the church was a seal of a true watchman of God. Like a fellow ministry worker once told us, "When we talk about Christ and salvation, donations to the ministry drop; but when we bring up the problems in the church, donations always increase."

Mix these two elements together and you find a powerful potion of talebearing and gossip. As scrupulous sentinels, we gather up every incredible tidbit of information we can get our hands on and set it afloat. We are constantly barraged with some of the most outrageous information—that never was true. Consider the time when I was conducting a week of prayer:

"That's it!" a brother in Christ exclaimed to me. "I appreciate everything you've been sharing, but this is the straw that breaks the camel's back!"

"What is it?" I queried.

"The General Conference President has gone to visit the pope," he retorted. "I can have nothing else to do with this church." (I must confess this caused me some concern, too.)

"Where did you get this information?" I asked.

"From a very reliable source who faithfully chronicles the latest apostasy in the Church."

"Well," I replied, "how do you know if it is true?"

"How do I know?" he defended. "It was printed in a newsletter and published for all to read!" (The implication was that if this information was published for all to read, it *must* be true.)

That was enough to shake me. "Could it be so?" I wondered to myself.

No sooner had I arrived back home than a full article addressing this rumor appeared in the *Review*. While frankly denying any such visit, our president made an earnest appeal to the independent ministry who had printed this false report to follow gospel order (see Matthew 18:15-17).

Some time later (at least two years) I was visiting in the home of some old church friends. In the course of our conversation, the Church and independent ministries came up. Then this very incident was used to justify pulling away from the Church. I felt it my duty at the time to confront my brother with the truth of the matter, in a kind and tactful way. But, much to my amazement, the truth made not the least bit of impact. The fact that this story had come from a ministry seen as conscientious, left no room in my brother's heart for a testimony of truth from our conference president, pleading with the Church to consider that he had been misrepresented.

I just wonder if this kind of loyalty to the *conscientious* brethren is not setting us up to be deceived. Don't misunderstand. I know that there is plenty to be concerned about in the Church. I am not suggesting here that we close our eyes to all our problems. What I am suggesting is a radical change in the manner in which we go about dealing with church problems. And I am suggesting it, not just for unity's sake, but for our own individual salvation's sake.

Would you be interested in some very plain counsel to help get us started in the right direction, even if it steps on all our toes a little? If a person comes to us with complaints, we should ask him, "Have you complied with the rules our Savior has given?" And if he has failed to carry out any particular of this instruction, do not listen to a word of his complaint. In the name and spirit of Jesus, refuse to take up a report against your brother or your sister in the faith. If members of the church go contrary to these rules, they make themselves subjects for church discipline, and should be under the censure of the church.

"Really!" you say, "Under church censure, just for complaining about our brethren?" I was quite amazed, too, especially since it was happening to me. The church board said that I was involved in a ministry that was highly critical of the Church and failing to follow Matthew 18:15-17. Try as I might then, in 1987, I saw no logic in their reasoning. I was just trying to keep people posted on all the Church's past and more current apostasies. Besides, it didn't seem right to be censured by a church that was not living up to all the light as I was. I felt they were the ones who should be censured, not me!

Now I realize that focusing on the failures of the church is one of Satan's most successful devices. By centering our attention upon each other's mistakes, repeating them again and again, Satan knows that we ourselves can receive only harm; for it is by beholding that we become changed (see 2 Corinthians 3:18).

The serpent is subtle! In his School of Deception he starts you off in basic "General Criticism—101."

This is the easy stuff—church leaders, obvious problems, clear or blatant apostasy.

Then you progress to "Detailed Criticism—102."

This is the harder stuff of doctrine and theology—fine points of truth that must be interpreted exactly the way I see it.

Inevitably he passes you on to "Destructive Criticism—103."

This turns you against the church body as a whole. Now you grasp at anything that will sustain your position against it. Little incidents, decades-old mistakes, hearsay and gossip. All are quickly taken in.

In this state you are just a step away from graduating to the enemy's final goal, "Self-Destructive Criticism—104."

Having partaken of the spirit of judging and criticizing to this degree, love will die out of the heart. Satan will lead you step-by-step to abandon your church, friends, and even the closest bonds of family. Now everyone and everything is consumed to feed the monster within. At this point, you are fully prepared to abandon Christianity in the testing-time before us, if not sooner, for you have imbibed the spirit of antichrist (see Romans 8:9; *Mount of Blessing,* p. 126). One of the very last tests for God's people, to gather warmth from the coldness of others, is now not even an option. The whole idea is repulsive to those who have been developing the character of Satan.

In my own experience with the church, I was somewhere between 102 and 103. I can relate best to Peter. When Christ warned that the disciples would all forsake Him, "Peter answered and said unto him, Though all men shall be offended because of thee, yet will I never be offended" (Matthew 26:33). Peter was honest and sincere, but self-deceived. He had no problem applying Christ's warning to his brethren because he was familiar with their faults and failures.

Peter might have thought, "I pray more than Matthew. I study harder than James or John. Jesus even proclaimed, before all the others, that the Father in heaven was teaching me. He never told them that" (see Matthew 16:17). (However, Christ also told Peter that the devil was teaching him, verse 23.)

"Oh, yes," we might say today, "I can see that those folks will never make it; they're just not committed enough. But me? I would never do that."

While Peter was honest in his statement, he did not know himself. He had been too busy comparing himself with the rest of the erring disciples instead of examining his own heart to see whether he was "in the faith" (2 Corinthians 13:5).

Christ urged him, and He urges us today: My faithful follower, instead of disparaging your brethren and thinking yourself stronger than they, "when thou art converted, strengthen thy brethren" (Luke 22:32). In saying this, Christ clearly implies that genuine heart-conversion is directly evidenced by "a spirit of meekness" toward erring brethren (see Galatians 6:1).

Are we listening to the warnings of our Savior, taking note of the defects in our own hearts? Or are we, like Peter, applying His warning to everyone else but ourselves? Undeniably, Peter's spirit is seen in many of us, who, when Christ warns us of our own weaknesses and danger, think that though all would forsake the Truth, "Yet will not I" (Mark 14:29). The powers of heaven stand ready to take from us the inclination to consider faultfinding a virtue. Are we willing to discern the enemy's snare and be set free from the weakness of our humanity?

CHAPTER SEVEN

The Beam That Blinds

I had just taken a seat in the rented hall when he approached me. He was quite intense, bursting forth in hard, straight tones, full of frustration. The authority of his manner made his argument seem unanswerable. "I do not feel that I can safely go to an organized church. I know I can't take someone else there. And I definitely can't support the Church financially, so why should I be a member?"

"Why, indeed?" I thought, though I knew exactly where he was coming from. I had just been there. "Please listen closely to the meeting tonight," I encouraged him. "It could be that you'll find an answer."

He did listen that night and the following day. The final evening he approached me again.

"I see it," he said with a calm, thankful voice.

"It's the negative mailings that I receive monthly," he continued. "If you focus on all the reports of apostasy in the Church, you can't help but want to separate from it."

"I can sympathize with what you have been going

through," I responded. "I've been fighting the same battle myself."

For the last few years I had spent much time taking in the latest apostasy rumors. Thinking myself to be a "watchman on the wall," I was reading material detailing the triumphs of the accuser of the brethren rather than the Author of our faith. It is easy to fall into the subtle illusion of thinking ourselves to be God's faithful watchmen while being totally misdirected as to what watchmen ought to be. But God was working a change for the better in me.

He led me to carefully study for my M.D. According to the Bible, the work of watchmen requires an M.D.—that's the "Master's Divinity," not college courses. This four-step degree is outlined succinctly in a Bible verse we glanced at earlier:

> *Brethren, if a man be overtaken in a fault, (1) ye which are spiritual, (2) restore such an one (3) in the spirit of meekness (4) considering thyself, lest thou also be tempted (Galatians 6:1).*

It was dawning on me that being *spiritual* does not mean wearing camel's hair and living in the wilderness. No doubt John the Baptist was a spiritual man. But his life was dedicated to reaching lost souls. He wasn't on some self-righteous ego trip like the scribes and Pharisees. And for sure, being spiritual does not consist in the outward appearance of righteousness. The Pharisees had that feature down pat, as well, yet were clueless when it came to reaching sinners. What's more, they didn't care, as long as they could claim Moses as their father (see John 9:28).

But Moses presents a clear, sublime example of the spirituality needed when working with the erring. Pleading with God after the golden calf apostasy, he put his own eternal salvation on the line as he sought forgiveness for those who had sinned. "Yet now, if thou wilt forgive their sin—; and if not, blot me, I pray thee, out of thy book which thou hast written" (Exodus 32:32). In reality, Moses was saying, "I'd rather be lost with them than saved without them."

This attitude of Moses is a reflection of our Savior. As Christ's bruised and bleeding body hung dying on the cross, suffering for our transgressions, He cried out, "My God, my God, why hast thou forsaken me?" (Matthew 27:46)

Why had God forsaken Him? Because He *would* not come down from the cross—not because He *could* not. It was not the metal spikes piercing the hands of Christ that held Him to that wooden beam of torture to bleed and die. His love held Him there. A tough, relentless love for wretched, ungrateful sinners bound Him to the cross to die of a broken heart that would not let us go. The cross that Christ was nailed upon, that took the life of God's dear Son, was not just a stake or man-made tree; it was mercy and forgiveness for you and me. Christ became one with sin that we might become one with Him.

This is the mystery of Christ's mission—personified.

Revelation 15 records the redeemed singing the song of *Moses* and the *Lamb* as the song of their own experience. All we need to do is look to Moses and the Lamb to understand this encounter. And when we do, we'll see this experience as a spiritual adventure in loving sinners while hating sin.

The apostle Paul exemplified this same element of reconciliation. In fact, his disposition toward his enemies is so unbelievable that before he explains it, he takes a whole verse to persuade us that he is telling the truth. "I say the truth in Christ, I lie not, my conscience also bearing me witness in the Holy Ghost, that I have great heaviness and continual sorrow in my heart. For I could wish that myself were accursed from Christ for my brethren, my kinsmen according to the flesh" (Romans 9:1-3).

In the Greek, the word for "accursed" is *anathema*, implying eternal separation from God. The amazing truth about this whole attitude is its object, the Jews, who hated Paul, to put it mildly. In fact, Paul gave an account of how much they despised him in 2 Corinthians 11:24, 25:

> *Of the Jews five times received I forty stripes save one.*
> *Thrice was I beaten with rods, once was I stoned,*
> *thrice I suffered shipwreck, a night and a day I have*
> *been in the deep.*

Let's do some quick math—five times forty is two hundred, subtract five, that leaves one hundred and ninety-five stripes on Paul's body. Then add the rods, stoning, and shipwreck. Can you comprehend the pain or picture the scars? If anyone had reason to get bitter about something, Paul did.

It kind of makes the old "That church isn't very friendly" line sink into insignificance.

John the beloved echoed Paul's same call to *Christ-like love* when he explained, "Hereby perceive we the love of God, because he laid down his life for us: and we ought to lay down our lives for the brethren" (1 John 3:16). He maintains that the possession of this love is how "we know that we have passed from death unto life" (1 John 3:14).

What? We are being asked to lay down our lives when the church is not functioning the way we believe it should? We are expected to be willing to taste eternal death for those whose theology we disagree with? Most of us would no doubt rather lay down our memberships than our lives. Have you ever noticed that it seems easier, at times, to love unbelievers than it is to love fellow church members? When John declares we pass from death to life by loving the brethren, he isn't kidding!

Jesus brings us to the same point in His sermon on the mount when He says:

"And why beholdest thou the mote that is in thy brother's eye, but considerest not the beam that is in thine own eye? Or how wilt thou say to thy brother, Let me pull out the mote out of thine eye; and, behold, a beam is in thine own eye? Thou hypocrite, first cast out the beam out of thine own eye; and then shalt thou see clearly to cast out the mote out of thy brother's eye" (Matthew 7:3-5).

Though the last three verses are somewhat figurative, the meaning is clear in the context of the gospel. The symbolic beam-in-the-eye syndrome is marked by a lack of self-sacrificing love, especially for our enemies (see Matthew 5:39-48).

Suddenly I was confronted with the idea that being spiritual involves a willingness to sacrifice myself, my opinions, my judgment, and even my eternal life in order to reach the erring. In stark contrast to this ideal, I faced a hollow reflection in my mirror—my great need stared back at me in glaring reality.

Catching glimpses of God and His undying love for humanity in the lives of Moses, Paul, and Christ, completely vanquished all excuses and human reasoning for separating from the Church. I felt undone, mistaken and impetuous. My plea was that of the psalmist, "Create in me a clean heart, O God; and renew a right spirit within me. . . . *Then* will I teach transgressors thy ways; and sinners shall be converted unto thee" (Psalm 51:10, 13).

On my journey back to the Church, the one thing I possessed was a great need. I rejoiced to realize the importance of loving the brethren. I was happy that the living substance of Christianity had pressed upon my self-righteous soul. Yet all my exuberance could not materialize the experience. It was just a beginning, the germinating embryo of a new attitude toward the Church.

I prayed, "Father in heaven, I now see that I have failed to have Your spirit, Your heart of love toward fellow sinners. I do not love the brethren as I know I should, as You do. My heart is full of criticism and judgment. You alone can change it. Father, take out the negative and replace it with the love of Jesus Christ. Remove the beam that blinds my vision, for Your glory and in Christ's name. Amen."

Now I was back on the right road. But my new direction was not to go unchallenged.

CHAPTER EIGHT

The Pointing Problem

This lady was obviously quite distressed. Almost in exasperation she vented the question that seemed to be disquieting her mind.

"Are you saying that we need to be perfect before we can rebuke the sins of others?" she asked.

(She was referring to the emphasis on loving the brethren considered in our last chapter). I was taken by surprise at her question. Her forthright approach and strong demeanor set me back. Yet considering the sublime character of God's love, there was only one answer that I could possibly give.

"No," I responded, "I am not saying that—God is."

Now, before you decide to close this book, allow me to clarify. To correct the sins of others and lead them to Christ, to reconcile the erring and look for the lost, is a work of the most sacred nature. Its consequences are eternal. The issues are life and death. We are called "ambassadors for Christ" (2 Corinthians 5:20). Our qualifications for this work must be of the highest order. Therefore, I put this question to you, as it really should be asked:

*Dare we take this work upon ourselves without the
love of Christ emanating from the depths of our being?*

I believe the answer to that question is: Never! Once we are
armed with the love of Christ, our efforts will be to "restore,"
not "condemn," the erring (see Galatians 6:1; John 3:17).

You see, after the fall of our first parents, we developed an
inbred problem, often glaring in its conduct, but not easily
acknowledged by us today. It came to light the very evening
Adam and Eve disobeyed the Lord. As they heard the voice
of God in the Garden, they felt their guilt and hid themselves
(see Genesis 3:8). The Lord's beckoning voice drew them out
and they immediately began to cast about for an explanation
as to why they were naked and afraid (see verses 9-11). Then
it happened. Failing to find a valid reason for his transgression, man pointed to woman. Then, coming under the close
scrutiny of her own guilt, woman pointed to snake (see verses
12, 13). And we've been pointing ever since (see Isaiah 58:9).

The spirit of mudslinging is in the very air we breathe. The
highest-rated daytime talk shows do it. The most popular ra-
dio personalities do it. Even our nation's political leaders do it.
It is everywhere and anyone is a target. The atmosphere of society today is polluted with sarcasm and criticism, which is why
Christians should be as a breath of fresh air. (Rush may be
right, but his attitude is not.)

Paul exhorts us "that, first of all," before we do any talking
about faults, "supplications, prayers, intercessions, and giving
of thanks, be made for all men; for kings, and for all that are
in authority" (1 Timothy 2:1, 2).

If Christ were here today, He might say, "Ye have heard that it hath been said," on every popular talk show, "Thou shalt love thy neighbor, and hate thine enemy. But I say unto you, Love your enemies, bless them that curse you, do good to them that hate you, and pray for them which despitefully use you, and persecute you" (Matthew 5:43, 44).

Praying for authority figures who misuse their positions presents a challenge. In addition, praying for our personal abusers poses a formidable test that threatens to undo us. Consider the story of Job.

God pointed to Job as His representative on earth. God called Job "perfect" and "upright" (see Job 1:1, 8). In context, Job's perfection is not to be found in his theology, but in his attitude of intercession and prayer. Job would rise early in the morning to pray for his children who seemed less committed than he, eating and drinking and possibly cursing God in their hearts (see Job 1:4, 5). In this way Job revealed the character of God who is continually interceding in behalf of sinners (see Hebrews 7:25).

Throughout the story, Satan worked through every possible avenue to discourage Job's attitude toward his fellow sinners and his God. He used economic trials, personal tragedy, ill health, friends and family. Job faltered from time to time, yet he maintained his faith. But notice the key to the whole story. "And the Lord turned the captivity of Job, when he prayed for his friends" (Job 42:10). Did you catch it? I hadn't. It was Job's spirit of prayer for the sinful and even for his self-appointed judges that was put to the test. His captivity finally turned as he *prayed* for his "miserable comforters" (see Job 16:2).

John the beloved was referring to this restorative-intercessory spirit when he wrote, "If any man see his brother sin a sin which is not unto death, he shall ask [pray], and he shall give him life for them that sin not unto death" (1 John 5:16).

The context of this verse is power-packed with assurance that God will hear and answer our petitions. "And this is the confidence that we have in him, that, if we ask any thing according to his will, he heareth us: And if we know that he hear us, whatsoever we ask, we know that we have the petitions that we desired of him" (verses 14, 15).

Hoping to dislodge our cold, self-centered prayers, God asks us to claim these prayer promises for those who are sinning. Humble, hopeful intercession for sinners may make all the difference between their salvation and their complete rejection of the Holy Spirit.

Satan seethes when a Christian prays like this. This self-sacrificing attitude of intercession irritates his senses like the sound of nails scraping a chalkboard. As illustrated by the story of Job, he works unceasingly to disrupt it. Often he is so successful that if the verse would have read, "When you see someone sin, gossip about it with others; use it as an excuse to do the same; or put it in a newsletter; write it in a book; sell it on a cassette tape or video," we might have little problem meeting the criteria.

It is not uncommon for the most conscientious and concerned of us to sometimes get so caught up in Isaiah 58, verse 1 ("Cry aloud, spare not, lift up thy voice like a trumpet, and shew my people their transgression, and the house of Jacob their sins"), that we leave off the rest of the chapter—verse 9, NIV, for example. (" 'If you do away with the yoke of oppression, with the pointing finger and the malicious talk.' ")

Without a context, we have a free-for-all: as long as the rebuke is straight, loud and clear on someone *else's* sins, it must be of God.

Solomon declared that "every way of a man is right in his own eyes: but the Lord pondereth the hearts" (Proverbs 21:2). We may be eager to straighten out others, quick to point out their mistakes, but slow to discern personal, individual failure in our representation of the spirit of Christ.

I am learning this in my own home. After I have delivered an important, intellectually-convincing lecture on the way things should be done, my wife will sometimes remind me that *the way* I have spoken undermines the strength of my logic. Perhaps we feel that strong voice tones or overbearing attitudes will help convince of our rightness. Maybe we think that if our logic doesn't work, the strength of our presentation will. Or it might be that we are just plain unaware of the way we come across. Having failed to study the grace and courtesy of Christ, our words are rash and impulsive.

Let the Holy Spirit unburden your conscience. Know that the victory Job gained by praying for his brethren is the victory we need in the church today. And the love that Job had for his children is the love that we need for our church family. It is the love that we need for each other and for the world.

CHAPTER NINE

Them and Us

Now might be as good a time as any to address another reason often brought up as evidence that the Church should not get our support. It is the idea that the Church is in apostasy, almost a given in some circles. Let's stop and analyze, for just a moment, what such a statement is saying. Sure, there are problems in the Church all over the world. In fact, I would have no argument with saying that there is apostasy in the Church, for it is in the very air we breathe. But we all understand that the Church is people—millions of people, to be a little more specific. And to say that the Church is in apostasy—besides being just plain exaggeration—is a pretty solemn judgment call to make on millions of people, most of whom we have never met.

When we talk about the Church being in apostasy, we might want to clarify. Obviously, we're talking about people and not buildings. If so, are we talking about *all* the people or just a sampling by which we presume to judge the rest? Without getting caught up in a "religious filibuster" (empty talk designed to sidetrack action on important issues), consider the following thoughts.

Have you ever noticed, based on Revelation 7:4-8, where those sealed are symbolized by the twelve tribes of Israel, that the tribe of Dan, one of the original twelve tribes, is missing (see Genesis 49:3-28)? This holds for us an important spiritual truth. The word *Dan* is defined in the Hebrew as "judge" and comes from a root which means, "to strive." Speaking prophetically of the "last days," Jacob described Dan as he that "shall judge his people" as "a serpent by the way, an adder in the path, that biteth the horse heels, so that his rider shall fall backward" (Genesis 49:1, 16, 17). That's a rather low character reference any way you look at it.

So Dan has been replaced by Manasseh, who was one of the sons of Joseph (see Genesis 48:20). Wanting to forget, and finally forgive, his brothers' cruel act in selling him as a slave, Joseph named his first son *Manasseh* (see Genesis 37:28; 41:51). It means, "causing to forget" and traces back in Hebrew to a root word which means "to forget, to remit, or to remove." This is the same definition as the Greek root for "forgive" as used in the New Testament (see John 20:23).

The lesson is simple and profound. No, the 144,000 in Revelation are not literal, male, Jewish virgins who convert to Christ and evangelize the world in the wake of the secret rapture. The sealed tribes represent the characters of the redeemed. The tribe of Dan is not among the sealed because it represents those who judge and criticize their brethren, underscoring these as disqualifying characteristics. Those who are ready to forgive, even as Joseph forgave the heartless sins of his brothers, will replace backbiters and accusers of the brethren.

Will we allow God to enable us to forgive and forget the sins of our brethren as Joseph did? Will we acknowledge with Joseph that God actually overrides every trial that comes to us? (See Genesis 45:5-8.) Will we, like the 195-stripe-beaten, thrice-rod-beaten, once-stoned, shipwrecked, apostle Paul, confess that "all things work together for good to them that love God, to them who are the called according to his purpose" (see Romans 8:28)?

Yes, there is apostasy in the Church. And the tendency can be to feel guilty-by-association when we see those in the Church who misrepresent Christianity. Some mishandle the Lord's money. Others hurt the Lord's children. In the Church are many who teach error and undermine our message and mission. True, we do not want to be accounted guilty of sanctioning sin, but neither should we become judgmental and pull away from the Church, discouraged by its problems. What can we do?

Consider two examples from the Bible. The first is Daniel. While he remained faithful to God during his nation's apostasy, Daniel still included himself with his unfaithful fellow countrymen. He believed in a corporate oneness expressed by the word "we." "We have sinned," said the faithful, righteous Daniel, "and have committed iniquity, and have done wickedly, and have rebelled, even by departing from thy precepts and from thy judgments" (Daniel 9:5).

If you think about it, that is a pretty amazing attitude to have toward a bunch of rebellious people. After all, if we were separated from our family and forced to march across hundreds of miles of desert to serve as a eunuch in the court of a cruel, heathen dictator, all because of the apostasy of our denomination, we'd probably be suing instead of praying.

"Wait a minute," I can hear someone say. "Perhaps Daniel didn't really mean for us to understand him in this way. He didn't really mean to include himself with all those terrible apostates. He didn't really mean to say *we*. It was an accident, a slip of the tongue, a modern translation."

Well, let's see if we can get some clarification from Daniel.

"Daniel, did you mean to say *we* when you mentioned your [denomi-]nation's apostasy or were you really meaning to say *they?*"

"*We* have sinned against thee" (Daniel 9:8, KJV).

"*We* have rebelled against him" (Daniel 9:9, KJV).

"Neither have *we* obeyed the voice of the Lord" (Daniel 9:10, KJV).

"*We* have sinned against him" (Daniel 9:11, KJV).

"*We* obeyed not his voice" (Daniel 9:14, KJV).

"*We* have done wickedly" (Daniel 9:15, KJV).

Thanks, Daniel.

Well, there we are. It's rather indisputable. Daniel put himself in the sinner's place, confessing sins of which he himself was not guilty. This experience is entirely different—in fact, it is in total opposition—from the natural heart. It points to a maturing of divine love that will constrain us to weep over the erring and those who have backslidden from God.

Daniel's attitude portrays something we desperately need today—an attitude of restoration rather than condemnation (see Galatians 6:1). When we see souls who are out of Christ, do we put ourselves in their place? Do we feel repentance before God in their behalf and work in this spirit to bring them to repentance? Even if they refuse to repent, are our hearts heavy because of their condition? Mine wasn't. Satan too often leads us to claim a pseudo perfection, which results in a "them and us" mentality. Daniel's attitude is the true goal of Christian perfection. Like our Savior, Daniel *"identified himself fully* with those who had fallen short of the divine purpose, confessing their sins as his own" (*Prophets and Kings,* p. 555; 2 Corinthians 5:21).

You may wonder, "Does it work?" Take a look at our second example, Ezra. When he entered into this attitude of intercessory prayer for his people, revival followed (see Ezra 9:3-6). Ezra did not afflict others; rather, he plucked off the hair of his own beard and head. Ouch! Nor did he bring up the problems in the church as a reason for neglecting his post of duty as Elijah had done in a time of weakness. (Paul describes Elijah as making "intercession to God *against* Israel" because this battle-worn prophet used his nation's apostasy as an excuse for separating from them. See Romans 11:2, 3.)

While Ezra stood firm against sin, he interceded *for* the sinner. Ezra's Christ-like efforts were not in vain (see Ezra 10:1). Not only was there weeping, but there was revival and reformation. The people turned from sin through the prayerful efforts of this man of God (see Ezra 10:11, 12).

Studying these lessons, my own heart sensed the need to identify with the weaknesses and failures of the church in the same way as did Daniel, Ezra and others. I could see that revival and reformation in the church are dependent upon more than just rebuking sin. I needed to confess the sins of my brethren as though they were my own, for they are, when I realize that "by the grace of God I am what I am" (1 Corinthians 15:10). Understanding the responsibility to restore the erring rather than condemn them, I saw my actions in a new light. And I began to view the church in a new light also.

I was beginning to realize, as never before, what the apostle Paul meant when describing the church as a body (1 Corinthians 12:12-27). In relation to Daniel's prayer, I now understood why, "whether one member suffer, all the members suffer with it" (1 Corinthians 12:26). Being part of the body, a member of the church, is not just intellectual ascent to doctrines; it is to be "tempered" together by God so that we have "the same care one for another" (1 Corinthians 12:24, 25). We don't close another member's probation, saying in our spirit and attitude, "I have no need of you" (see 1 Corinthians 12:21). We don't pull away from the body, saying, "I'm afraid to be reckoned with you." Instead we dare to be like Daniel, interceding for the church family, identifying ourselves with them and trusting God for the results.

CHAPTER TEN

Sons of Thunder

I once read a story of an honest, dedicated Christian who wrote a tract entitled, *Come to Jesus.* The tract became famous and brought many souls to Christ. Some time later this man got caught up in theological dispute. He responded to a publication from an opponent by writing an article filled with denunciation as sharp and cutting as a razor. Looking for a title, he solicited his friend. His friend wisely suggested: "Call it *Go to the Devil* by the author of *Come to Jesus.*" He destroyed the article.

This story describes something that had crept into my heart as I battled for the truth. It was a "manliness" of the world's order, revealing a denunciatory, cutting, demeaning spirit toward anyone who might challenge my view of rightness. It was a "sons of thunder" attitude (see Mark 3:17).

This was the nickname for James and John, two of Christ's disciples. It was a name they "lived up to" on more than one occasion—like the time Christ sought a night's lodging in a Samaritan village while making His last journey to Jerusalem.

Samaritans and Jews were bitter enemies, the main contention being the issue of worship (see John 4:20). Being descendants of Jacob, the Samaritans had built a rival temple of worship in Samaria and were looking for the coming Messiah (see John 4:12, 25).

Contrary to the teaching of the Pharisees, Christ ministered to the Samaritans. Yet He still maintained that the Jews had been entrusted with the truth about salvation (see John 4:22). This prejudiced the Samaritans (see Luke 9:51). So, on this last journey to Jerusalem, the Samaritans jealously refused to provide Jesus a place to rest for the night, "because His face was as though He would go to Jerusalem" (Luke 9:53).

Into this situation, as on cue, came James and John, the "sons of thunder." Convinced that the Samaritans had gone too far, they became judge, jury, and executioner. Like most of us today, they felt a solemn obligation to defend the truth—in this case, the Truth incarnate in human flesh (see John 14:6). Being faithful Bible students, the experience of Elijah came promptly to their minds. As that devoted prophet was confronted by soldiers of wicked King Ahab, Elijah called fire down from heaven, not once, but twice, to consume them (see 2 Kings 1:10, 12).

These disciples were passionately persuaded. How much *more* must the Son of God Himself be worthy of such retaliation! There was only one course of action to take. And it wasn't diplomacy!

Responding to the affront, they pressed for reprisal: "Lord, wilt Thou that we command fire to come down from heaven, and consume them, even as Elias did?" (Luke 9:54). This was actually a recommendation disguised as a question. In modern day vocabulary— "Surely You now see what great sinners these Samaritans really are! They don't deserve Your efforts. They just deserve to burn!" (See Revelation 20:9.)

The self-righteous denunciation had barely escaped the lips of these offended disciples when Jesus turned and "rebuked them, and said, Ye know not what manner of spirit ye are of. For the Son of man is not come to destroy men's lives, but to save them" (Luke 9:55, 56). That must have hit hard! Imagine being rebuked by the very person you seek to protect and honor. What a challenge to have the right truth and the wrong spirit.

In a very real sense, I felt that this same rebuke justly fell upon me. All the right doctrines, but the wrong spirit. This was our confession, Ty's and mine, given to a group of pastors and church leaders at our local Upper Columbia Conference in 1990. Most of them seemed surprised. A few were very skeptical. But who could blame them?

For the last four or five years, we had been an independent ministry, somewhat critical of the church. All of a sudden we called them requesting a meeting. Then, without dropping much of a clue as to our purpose, we poured forth a confession of truth laid upon our hearts by the convicting power of the Holy Spirit. We had previously given up hope for the Conference, judging them as untrustworthy apostates. While we had faith, truth and prophecy, we did not believe or hope all things concerning our church leadership (see 1 Corinthians 13:1, 2, 7). Convicted by the Holy Spirit that this attitude was wrong, we now confessed our fault to the brethren (see James 5:16).

This was the start of a new relationship with our church that we have always regretted not doing sooner. But even then it did not come without struggle. Warnings sounded from various independent quarters not to work with the leadership. "They'll shut you down or control you," we were advised.

Disregarding such instruction brought some heavy rumors. It was said that we had been NLP (neurolinguistic programming)-hypnotized and Jesuit-infiltrated. Perhaps some just needed to justify their position or maybe they truly believed it. What mattered at the time was that we knew it wasn't true. God had clearly dictated through His Word the course we were to pursue (see Psalm 32:8). Whatever the consequences, we would follow His principles. We could do nothing else.

We were now one of over one hundred supportive ministries of the church. Is that different from an independent one? Positively. Without going into detail, there are three basic principles that differentiate supportive ministries from independent ministries:

- Communication (Acts 15:2, 6)
- Cooperation (Acts 15:25-28)
- Accountability (Acts 15:1, 24)

1) Supportive ministries communicate regularly and in a positive way with church leadership, whether it concerns church problems or new insights into Bible truth. 2) They also cooperate with the goals and basic mission of the church. And, 3) they place themselves in a position of accountability to the church.

As with the Samaritans' treatment of Christ, we, too, may experience economic boycott or even physical harm at the hands of religionists whose worship differs from ours (see Revelation 13:7, 15-17). Our response to persecution will be a test of the depth of our religious experience (see Revelation 13:10). No matter what our profession, even if we are allied with the truth, a wrong spirit is a denial of Christ. It is a revelation of the dragon-like spirit of Satan.

The true test comes in the face of our worst enemies (see Matthew 24:10-14). Meekness means to have a tender and humble spirit full of love and compassion. Erring on the side of mercy is its preference (see Luke 6:36). Treating even your bitterest enemies with respect and deference is its power (see Matthew 17:27). Yoking up with Christ is its source (see Matthew 11:28-30).

Slowly but surely I was learning—according to Galatians 6:1—that "the erring can be restored in *no other way* than in the spirit of meekness, gentleness, and tender love" (*Testimonies for the Church,* vol. 2, p. 52).

Our journey from an independent ministry to a supportive ministry presented many challenges. Yet the spiritual principles awakened in our hearts were both strong confirmation and sweet compensation. We were confident God had guided us back to His remnant church. Our trust was in Him.

Through practical application of these sublime truths, we lost over half of our ministry's support base. Hoping that we were as honest and sincere as we believed those previous supporters had been, we looked for continual verification which always seemed to come at the right time.

CHAPTER ELEVEN

Harsh Words from Martin Luther

From posters in New York subways to bulletin boards on Oregon highways, the message was getting out—"The pope is the Antichrist"—bold and straight. People were astir. Some were outraged. Others apologetic. I heard that one person even joined our church.

The plan originated with a layman who had gained quite a reputation, as well as a small following in our church circles. He had done a good work in printing an illustrated edition of *The Great Controversy*. However, a careful reading of the book would have shown him that placing placards all over the country denouncing the pope was not a successful approach (see *The Great Controversy*, pp. 224, 225).

This story describes another issue I had to work through in coming back to God's remnant church. It had to do with the presentation of the three angels' messages, or what I thought was a *lack* of presentation. I felt that the church was toning it down, compromising the truth for fear of persecution. I know this is a major factor with many today, not only because of my own experience, but also due to the above-mentioned incident, which caused division in many churches, as well as an entire conference. This was because many members wanted to support this method of outreach. Yet others knew God had counseled us against making harsh, denunciatory thrusts at other denominations.

All the commotion among the brethren prompted a response of this brother in a newsletter to his supporters. Under a section entitled "HARSH WORDS" he attempted to justify his spirit and approach. The main thrust of his defense was: God led Martin Luther to bring reformation to the world in the sixteenth century; if you think I'm harsh, listen to him. And then followed excerpts from the writings of Luther:

> *I am unable to pray without at the same time cursing. If I am prompted to say, "Hallowed be Thy name," I must add, "Cursed, damned, outraged be the name of the papists.* . . . . *I never work better than when I am inspired by anger"* (Will and Ariel Durant's II Volume, History of Civilization, Volume VI: The Reformation, p. 418).

"But," you say, "God used Martin Luther in a mighty way." True, God used Luther to ignite the reformation. The question is, can we justify our course of action by following Luther's method today? My Bible tells me, *No!* It is not Martin Luther, but Christ whom we should follow (see John 10:27; Revelation 14:4).

Looking to the example of finite men as justification for our wrong attitudes is nothing new. In Christ's day, James and John tried to justify their harsh attitude toward the Samaritans by quoting from the past experience of Elijah (see Luke 9:51-56). In our day, we quote from Martin Luther. As we cogitate upon this tendency and prayerfully consider its repercussions, we will see the error in following such a course.

Men who are harsh and censorious often excuse or try to justify their lack of Christian politeness because some of the Reformers worked with such a spirit, and they claim that the work for this time requires the same spirit; but this is not so. God did not select the Reformers because they were overbearing, passionate men. He accepted them as they were, notwithstanding these traits of character; but He would have placed tenfold greater responsibilities upon them had they been of humble mind, having their spirits under control of reason.

The Bible teaches that the example of men should only be followed as they "imitate Christ" (1 Corinthians 11:1, NKJV). Yet even here we should be cautious. We may be tempted to point to Christ's stern rebukes of the Pharisees to justify our harshness. And it is true that Christ Himself did not suppress one word of truth. We must remember, though, He spoke truth always in love.

Throughout His life He exercised the greatest tact, and thoughtful, kind attention in His intercourse with the people. He was never rude, never needlessly spoke a severe word, never gave needless pain to a sensitive soul. He did not censure human weakness. He fearlessly denounced hypocrisy, unbelief and iniquity, but tears were in His voice as He uttered His scathing rebukes.

Self-justification may be a sure sign that we are in the wrong, especially when it concerns a lack of Christ-likeness. When self-justification takes the place of God's justification, we point to the faults of others to prop ourselves up. In this way we deceive ourselves into thinking we are better than we actually are (2 Corinthians 10:12).

If any instruction in the Bible is clear, it is that "the servant of the Lord must not strive; but be gentle unto all men, apt to teach, patient. In meekness instructing those that oppose themselves; if God peradventure will give them repentance to the acknowledging of the truth; and that they may recover themselves out of the snare of the devil, who are taken captive by him at his will" (2 Timothy 2:24-26).

At this point you may be wondering, "What about righteous indignation? That's what Christ had when He cleansed the temple."

Fair enough. Some circumstances today might call for more exercise of this godly trait. Nevertheless, before we justify our fearless rebukes as righteous *revelations,* consider some advice from the Bible on the subject.

The book of James has much to say about outward actions revealing an inward faith: "Wherefore, my beloved brethren, let every man be swift to hear, slow to speak, slow to wrath. For the wrath of man worketh not the righteousness of God" (James 1:19, 20).

The practical import of these Scriptures is found in the Greek definition of *wrath,* which is "justifiable abhorrence." God cautions us to be slow to manifest a righteous *revelation* because it may not be best for bringing sinners to salvation. Indignation is what the guilty expect. They are prepared for it.

But kind forbearance takes them by surprise and often awakens their better impulses and arouses a longing for a nobler life.

The apostle Paul boils the question down to one of two options:

- What is lawful for us?
- What will edify others?

"All things are lawful for me," he declares, "but all things are not expedient: all things are lawful for me, but all things edify not" (1 Corinthians 10:23).

Even though our indignation be righteous and, therefore, lawful, a demonstration of it is not always best; it does not always work for edification.

Ponder for a moment the example of our Savior in relation to the death of Lazarus. Christ arrived at the grave site of His friend. He read the hearts of all those who were assembled. He saw what no one else could, that in many, what passed as a demonstration of grief, was only pretense. He knew that some in the company, then displaying hypocritical sorrow, would soon be planning to kill, not only Himself, but the one they appeared to be sorrowing for. In that moment Christ could have stripped from them their robes of pretended sorrow. But He restrained His righteous indignation.

The Bible records that He "groaned in the spirit and was troubled" (see John 11:33). The word *groaned* means "to have indignation." Christ's spirit was indignant but He restrained the outward display of this righteous indignation.

Christ's example in this instance teaches us that the purpose of reproof is not to vent our indignation, but to save souls.

Even righteous indignation should be concealed or revealed in relation to the best way of reaching the hearts of all those involved. A kind, silent act of humility, like Christ's washing of the disciples' feet, is an unspoken rebuke that often speaks louder than words.

The point is that a rebuke in the form of humility may speak more clearly than a loud denunciation. In this regard the following concept had a profound effect upon my own approach to the erring:

We may never know, until the judgment, the influence of a kind, considerate course of action on the inconsistent, the unreasonable, and unworthy. If, after a course of provocation and injustice on their part, you treat them as you would an innocent person, you even take pains to show them special acts of kindness, then you have acted the part of a Christian; and they become surprised and ashamed, and see their course of action and meanness *more clearly* than if you plainly stated their aggravated acts to rebuke them.

Yes, how to reach those in error was a major hurdle for me concerning the church. At times I felt as if they were afraid to share the message of warning, fearful to call sin by its right name. Yet, now I see that they had the difficult job of discerning between tact and compromise. When it comes to reaching hearts in the world and in the church, finding the right measure of truth and love may always be a challenge.

We live in "perilous times" because many have "a form of godliness" and are "denying the power thereof" (2 Timothy 3:1, 5). I was learning, however, not to infer from this that we need to be harsher than the Reformers. In reality we need more of the spirit of meekness than ever before.

CHAPTER TWELVE

I Did It Uzza's Way

It is one of those divine judgment stories that can leave you wondering about the character of God. In fact, the account of Uzza has troubled many people.

The story begins with a great revival that was taking place in Israel. The plan was to bring the ark of God back to the nation, an idea that "was right in the eyes of all the people" (1 Chronicles 13:3, 4). The law of God had been neglected, the counsel of God's word ignored. Captains, leaders, people and priests all agreed on one point, that the nation needed revival and reformation. (See 1 Chronicles 13:1, 2.)

It is the same today. In the last few years I have visited with numerous pastors and conference workers. Almost without exception each one has revealed a desire for revival and reformation. None has ever denied that there are grave problems among us. The issue boils down to one simple question— HOW? Back to Uzza.

And so, as the story goes, "they carried the ark of God in a new cart out of the house of Abinadab: and Uzza and Ahio drave the cart. And David and all Israel played before

God with all their might, and with singing, and with harps, and with psalteries, and with timbrels, and with cymbals, and with trumpets. And when they came unto the threshingfloor of Chidon, Uzza put forth his hand to hold the ark; for the oxen stumbled. And the anger of the Lord was kindled against Uzza, and He smote him, because he put his hand to the ark: and there he died before God" (1 Chronicles 13:7-10).

Zap! He's history. At least that's our view, one that leads many to become like David who was "afraid of God that day" (1 Chronicles 13:12). Still, I am personally persuaded, as David may have been in time, that God did not allow Uzza to perish without doing everything possible to save him. "The Lord . . . is longsuffering to us-ward, not willing that any should perish, but that all should come to repentance" (2 Peter 3:9). When this verse is placed before the numerous judgments found in the Old Testament, we find the balance of God's justice and love. We may not understand all the reasons for God's actions concerning Uzza, but we do know that God loved him (see John 3:16).

Yet there are some insights into this story that can benefit us today. The most significant is found in 1 Chronicles 15 where David states his realization as to why this "first" effort for reformation was not of God. "The Lord our God made a breach upon us, for that we sought Him *not after the due order*" (1 Chronicles 15:13).

Here we hit upon the theme of our study—HOW to bring revival and reformation to others. David acknowledges that in the first attempt to bring the law to the people "we did not inquire of Him about *how* to do it in the prescribed way" (1 Chronicles 15:13, NIV).

It seems that Uzza should have known this, too, for none perish without being given opportunity to receive light and understanding (see James 4:17). But like many of us, Uzza had a strong personality. (*Uzza* means "strength.") He wanted to bring revival his way, so he put the ark on a new cart and "drave the cart" (1 Chronicles 13:7). A new cart, pulled by strong oxen and driven forward by a strong man, would have moved quite rapidly.

God had designed that the ark be carried by men on foot, requiring a much slower pace. These men were to be especially chosen by God for this special ministry (see 1 Chronicles 15:2). God must have tried to communicate this to Uzza. Perhaps the threshingfloor of Chidon was one of His many attempts to slow Uzza down a bit, but he wouldn't listen. Instead of responding to the still small voice of the Holy Spirit, Uzza rashly put forth his hand to steady the ark.

Here is where God could do no more to reach Uzza's heart. He had tried everything to help Uzza realize that this was not God's way, not His "due order" of bringing His law, the standard of truth, back to the people. Then Uzza put forth his hand, seemingly to protect God's law from falling, but in reality he was trying to protect himself, his way, his ideas, and his purposes at all costs.

We face a similar danger today. With the great need for revival and reformation in our midst, we may attempt to bring the standard of God's law to the church in our own way and not in God's way. We want to move fast, running ahead of the Lord. It can be easy to drive and push, using the strength of our character more than relying on the moving of the Holy

Spirit. I did this and was sure that I was in the right, when in truth I had rejected the "due order" of God, the "way" of Jesus Christ (see 1 Chronicles 15:13; John 14:6).

Satan's object is accomplished just as surely when men run ahead of Christ and do the work He has never entrusted to their hand, as when they remain in the Laodicean state, lukewarm, feeling rich and increased with goods, and in need of nothing. The two classes are equally stumbling blocks.

One of the clearest revelations that Uzza's approach paralleled my very attitude came during a seminar in a small church. Between presentations the head elder took me aside. In short order he explained the philosophy of his little church. "This is a conservative church," he said, believing I would appreciate what was coming. "We preach it straight here and if people don't like it, they know where the door is—they can just leave."

I was stunned. Yet this elder had only described frankly and succinctly my own approach. "Preach the truth and let the chips fall where they may."

It is in this way that I, like Uzza, was in "error" (2 Samuel 6:7). But God was merciful. In the words of the apostle Paul: "I thank Christ Jesus our Lord, who hath enabled me, for that he counted me faithful, putting me into the ministry; Who was before a blasphemer, and a persecutor, and injurious: but I obtained mercy, because I did it ignorantly in unbelief. And the grace of our Lord was exceeding abundant with faith and love which is in Christ Jesus" (1 Timothy 1:12-14).

Perhaps my experience was not quite as bad as Paul's. After all I didn't exactly haul anyone off to jail. Yet the seriousness of my position against God's church was the same. Can any greater delusion deceive the human mind than that which leads men to indulge a self-confident spirit, to believe that they are right and in the light, when they are drawing away from God's people, and their cherished light is darkness?

How can we learn from Uzza's error today? The most impressive lesson is to understand that God has a "due order" for bringing revival to His people.

Like Uzza, some of us may have strong personalities. We are anxious to bring the law to the people even if we do it in the wrong way. We need God's help to let His due order for reformation take precedence over our fallible ideas. That old Sinatra favorite, "I Did It My Way," was Uzza's theme song, and it may be ours, too, if we fail to follow carefully the way of Jesus Christ (see John 14:6).

CHAPTER THIRTEEN

The Perfect Conflict

This chapter explains yet another important issue that played a part in my separating from the church. Mind you, I was tempted to leave this chapter out because the topic has been debated so much. In fact, it is probably one of the most recurrent conflicts discussed in the history of Christiandom. It has impacted our lives, families and churches like no other subject has. It is a misunderstanding of what Christ *really meant* when He said, "Be ye therefore perfect, even as your Father which is in heaven is perfect" (Matthew 5:48).

I still remember a brother who got caught up, for a time, in a group advocating sinlessness. During some exchanges with us, he unwittingly bore false witness. Picking up on his transgression, we pressed him on the point, attempting to show him that he was not as sinless as he thought himself to be (see 1 John 1:8). But in order to protect his doctrine of perfection, he denied breaking the ninth commandment. Not until he had left the group did he later confess to trying to conceal his sin.

Then there was the prayer meeting I accidentally attended with an offshoot group. It was taught that John 17:9—"I pray not for the world, but for them which thou hast given me"—meant that they were not to pray for anyone, family included, who had not accepted their doctrine of sinlessness.

On another occasion my wife and I were told that our probation was closed because we could not agree with a certain view of overcoming sin. Later the person admitted that this was a scare tactic used to coerce people into accepting their doctrine of instantaneous perfection.

Too often the whole focus of being perfect translates into merely *acknowledging* that we can have victory over every sin. That bottom line rests on our theological profession. We *say* that we can overcome all sin. Then we fight for that profession with all our might, at any cost. As long as we are professing and fighting for that profession, we are convinced we're in the right camp.

Yet how shallow is our profession when we talk about being perfect and are less than merciful in our attitude toward the erring. We try to make people *admit* that they can overcome all sin through God's grace, while manifesting critical words, impatience, anger and attitudes unbeffitting to followers of Jesus Christ. This is a denial by our actions of the very truth advocated with our words.

Christ said, *"Be ye."* He did not say to profess to be, argue about being, try to prove you are being, or force others to be. He simply said, "Be ye."

In the words of Nike—"Just do it!"

In other words, it is not essential for you to know and *tell others* all the whys and wherefores of what constitutes the new heart, or the position they can and must reach so as never to sin. You have no such work to do.

In writing to the church at Philippi, the apostle Paul aimed some important counsel and encouragement toward each individual working out his *"own* salvation with fear and trembling," in tandem with God working in the heart.

Fulfilling the fourteen words of Matthew 5:48 has more to do with how we treat people who mistreat us than with doctrinal tenet (see Matthew 5:38-48). Moving beyond theological argument, we come to see their "real meaning."

If we would represent Christ's character by obeying Matthew 5:48, there would be a great change in evildoers. Many souls would be convicted of their sinfulness and converted *by our refusal to resent the evil actions of those controlled by satanic agencies.* We must prayerfully and determinedly work on the Lord's side. In all the issues that provoke the soul we should resist the evil and refuse to abuse the evildoer.

Being perfect as God is perfect means refusing to be overcome by evil, and by overcoming "evil with good" (Romans 12:21). It calls for the exercise of mercy in our daily relations with one another because it is "by mercy," as well as truth, that "iniquity is purged" (Proverbs 16:6). Perhaps this is why Luke extends the Matthew 5 reference on perfection with the words, "be ye therefore merciful, as your Father also is merciful" (Luke 6:36). The point remains that mercy and perfection are two sides of the same coin.

Ultimately the real issue of being perfect comes down to one very practical truth—how we relate to fellow sinners. Are we working to restore the erring in a spirit of meekness or just trying to prove them wrong? (See Galatians 6:1.) Are we trying to win souls or win arguments? If intellectual enlightenment is our main objective, we are in trouble. Those whom Christ commends in the judgment may have known little of theology, but they have cherished His principles (see Romans 2:1-29).

Like the Jews, we can claim to be "a guide of the blind, a light of them which are in darkness, an instructor of the foolish, a teacher of babes," and have only "the form of knowledge and of the truth in the law" (Romans 2:19, 20). We may boast in our theology, and ramble on endlessly about perfection; but, as the following poem so adequately expresses, we may be quietly surprised when we get to heaven. (Pardon the theology.)

I dreamed death came the other night and heaven'
gates swung wide
With kindly grace an angel ushered me inside
And there to my astonishment stood folks I'd known
on earth;
Some I judged and labeled—"unfit" or "of little worth."
Indignant words came to my lips, but never were set free
For every face showed stunned surprise; no one
expected me.

C.R. Hembree

Think about it this way: the devils "believe and tremble" (James 2:19). What do the devils believe? Do they believe that Christ is the Son of God? Do they believe that He is coming again soon? Indeed they do, but will they be saved for all their believing? No. And neither will we if we are void of "the Spirit of Christ," because without His spirit we are "none of His" (Romans 8:9). Consequently, there will be many in heaven who had wrong theology—and the right spirit. But there will be none in heaven who had all the right theology—and the wrong spirit.

Please do not conclude from anything I have said that we

cannot be perfect. In fact, our church history reveals the story of a man who was said to have found the key to being perfect and never falling. Sounds haughty, huh? You may be surprised.

The story goes back many years to Topsham, Maine. Sabbath keepers met for worship in the large kitchen of Brother Stockbridge Howland. One particular morning Brother Howland, with his face aglow, proclaimed, "Brethren, I have found it. I have found that we can pursue a course of action regarding which the guarantee of God's word is: 'Ye shall never fall.' And I am going to tell you about it."

He then began to tell them of one of the members, a poor fisherman, who felt that he was not as respected as he thought he should be and that other members thought themselves above him. This was not the case, but to the fisherman, it was. So Brother Howland went to the fisherman's house and knelt before him saying:

"My brother, forgive me. What is it that I have done?"

The man took his visitor by the arm and tried to raise him to his feet.

"No," said Brother Howland, "What have you against me?"

"I have nothing against you," the fisherman responded.

"But you must have," said Brother Howland, "because once we could speak to one another; but now you do not speak to me at all, and I want to know what is the matter."

"Get up, Brother Howland," the fisherman implored.

"No," said Brother Howland, "I will not."

"Then I must get down," the fisherman declared, and he fell on his knees, and confessed how childish he had been and how many evil surmisings he had cherished.

"And now," he said, "I will put them all away."

It is said that, as Brother Howland told of this experience, his face shone with the glory of the Lord.

From this story we find the real meaning of perfection. The question to ponder is not, "Can we be perfect?" but rather, "What does it really mean to be perfect?" If Christ is waiting with longing desire for the perfection of His character in His people, then perfection of character must be possible or His mission will never be accomplished. But His mission *will* be "finished" (see Revelation 10:7). When? When we love His world as He has loved it, then for us His mission is realized. We are fitted for heaven; for we have heaven in our hearts.

Christ's mission is accomplished when we accept His divine love and refuse to allow the prevailing apostasy to prompt us to unchristian feelings and actions toward the world, even if it is in the church. When, through His mercy, we have a love that will not "wax cold" because "iniquity abounds," then the gospel will go to the entire world *as a witness* to all nations and the end will come (see Matthew 24:12, 14).

The example of Brother Howland was the course Light Bearers Ministry pursued toward our local conference. Humbling ourselves to confess our evil surmisings and hard feelings against the conference officials opened the door for the unity we now cherish. As we left that initial meeting, one of the conference men drew close to us. In humble, sincere tones, he said, "When we went into that room I considered you my enemies. Now I see you as my brothers in Christ."

It has worked in church history past and it is working in church history present. I am persuaded that this spirit of humility and love will work for you, too. But beware! All your bitterness will disappear before your very eyes. Just so you know.

CHAPTER FOURTEEN

Final Thoughts

They were two telephone calls within minutes of each other.

She was lamenting the fact that no one in the church would write to her son, who was in prison.

He was complaining that our satellite evangelism was a waste of effort, since we weren't preaching the truth.

They were both struggling souls, but they came from completely opposite ends of the spectrum.

"I can't go to church without leaving in tears," she exclaimed. "I've resigned all my positions and I'm about ready to withdraw my membership!"

"Our church is not preaching the message," he charged. "None of our leaders are genuine Christians and they don't deserve our financial support!"

She said there was no love.

He said there was no truth.

The very next day, God answered her needs by providentially putting us in contact with a church member, with thirteen years' experience in prison ministry, who lived in the same state as her son's prison.

This final chapter is dedicated to answering the struggles of the second caller and for any other hurting souls out there wrestling with the failures of the church.

It transpired not long ago in a small church in London, England, though it could have occurred anywhere. In fact, I am sure it is an oft-repeated incident in the world church.

A new person—she had just been attending church for a short time—was approached by another member. As they entered into friendly conversation, the member pointed to other members of the church. Then, in a confiding tone, she said, "These people are not really Seventh-day Adventists. I can take you to some meetings where you will find real Seventh-day Adventists."

In this particular case the new attendee was not sure how to respond. Her familiarity with the Bible was not as developed as she needed. But a thought was impressed upon her mind:

"Christ said that the wheat and the tares are to grow together until the harvest," she responded.

"Oh," came a surprised reply. And that was the end of that.

This new convert was baptized, or I should say, rebaptized, a few weeks later. She is my twin sister, returning, after some years of absence, to God's remnant church. As she recounted this incident to me, she exclaimed that focusing on people and their faults had been the very reason she had left the church in the first place.

My sister had gotten stymied by the problems in the church. The whole emphasis ended up leading her back to the world. Of course, this is not everyone's experience. Some go to other religious faiths. I never went back to the world, but I did leave the church denomination in spirit. Eventually I was disfellowshipped, which is another story; then was finally reconciled and rebaptized in 1991. Being censured is not something I care to boast about or even like to admit. But I desire to help those who, like myself, may struggle with the concept of the "true church."

Over the years I've observed a cycle. When people come to the realization of the truth for the first time, whether new converts or even lifelong Adventists, they are zealous in their faith. Satan moves right in to get their focus away from soul-winning, for he knows they will be a power in the Lord's hands. Some are lulled to sleep by the Laodicean dirge:

"You're hot and zealous now, but you'll cool down like the rest of us in time."

He takes others into offshoot movements. Many, like myself and now my sister, make a full circle (praise God!). Others aren't so fortunate. The Bible warns of this danger just prior to the second coming of Christ:

"And let us consider one another to provoke unto love and to good works: Not forsaking the assembling of ourselves together, as the manner of some is; but exhorting one another: and so much the more, as ye see the day approaching" (Hebrews 10:24, 25).

This verse maintains that we can resist the present end-time tendency to forsake church-assembly by provoking each other unto love and good works, rather than faultfinding. As never before, we need help in this area. Consider the experience I had some time ago.

It was late Friday night somewhere in the eastern states. As

I lay in bed thinking about the next day's presentations, I heard some noise just outside the bedroom door of the home where I was staying. There were a few voices and what sounded like some quiet laughing. Unable to sleep due to being wired-up from the evening meeting, I decided to investigate on my way to the bathroom. Meandering quietly toward the family room, I discovered my host and a friend watching a video.

They were so engrossed, they hardly noticed my presence. I was curious to find out what was worth watching at such a late hour on Sabbath. It didn't take long to figure out. The video was about the latest apostasy happening in the church. And sure enough, every now and then one or the other of them would snicker or grin. Of course, they couldn't help themselves, considering the sarcastic, near-comical manner in which the speaker defamed the church. I would have had a hard time keeping a straight face, too, except that I quickly turned away and went back to my room.

Resisting a cynical attitude toward problems in the church can be difficult at times. To hope all things, believe all things and endure all things, especially toward the disobedient, who may be persecuting us, is a high calling. Even David, a man after God's own heart, struggled with envying the prosperity of the wicked.

"They are not in trouble as other men; neither are they plagued like other men," he bemoaned (Psalm 73:5). Not until he saw their final end in sanctuary symbolism did he realize how foolish he was in holding hard feelings against them (see Psalm 74:17-22). Then his heart was grieved and his conscience stricken. He learned in symbolism what his successor-son, Solomon, later learned by experience: "the way of transgressors is hard" (Proverbs 13:15). According to the Bible, we don't need to add our two cents to those who are destined to feel God's wrath (see Romans 12:14-21).

By consistently placing before us an example of behavior and attitude in all things, Christ unveiled the way to overcome our tendency to become bitter toward the erring and even our persecutors. First of all, He explains that persecution is a blessing that *should* cause us to "rejoice, and be exceeding glad," not to be bitter and get exceedingly angry. It's supposed to indicate that we're on the same path as God's faithful of old (see Matthew 5:11, 12), though the fact that we do get angry is a sure indication that we're not.

Actually, contrary to popular persecution rationale, undergoing persecution does not necessarily mean that you are doing what is right. The Bible says, "all that will live godly in Christ Jesus shall suffer persecution" (2 Timothy 3:12). It does not say that all those who suffer persecution are living godly in Christ Jesus. Sometimes we bring persecution upon ourselves (see 1 Corinthians 13:3).

But here's the point. Just before His cruel crucifixion at the hands of the religious leaders, our Savior approached Jerusalem. And instead of fanning bitter thoughts toward his enemies, He wept for them (see Luke 19:41). The people lauding Him with praise must have been shocked. Why was their newly crowned King weeping so mournfully? They would have been even more shocked to know that the source of His sorrow came from His projected view of the fate of Jerusalem and of the whole world. As He looked beyond His own imminent pain, any thought of anger or ill will toward His persecutors was neither an option nor a temptation. Uppermost in His mind was the final destination of His unmerciful accusers and of us.

"Weep not for me, but weep for yourselves, and for your children," Christ compassionately rebuked the weeping women as He carried His cross to Golgotha (Luke 23:28). And He meant it! "For, behold, the days are coming, in the which they shall say, Blessed are the barren, and the wombs that never bare, and the paps which never gave suck. Then shall they begin to say to the mountains, Fall on us; and to the hills, Cover us" (Luke 23:29, 30; see also Revelation 6:14-17). How sorrowful Christ felt—for them! Though He was about to be heartlessly and unjustly crucified, His thoughts were only of our anguish and suffering.

This is why Jesus wept over Jerusalem. The very depths of His being were broken up by the sin of Israel's rejection of their Messiah. Tears of unutterable, irrepressible agony and grief came from the heart of Jesus for us, who hated Him without a cause.

We need that heart.

We can have that heart. The final destiny of the wicked is a strong motivation to inspire reconciliation, even to the point of death (see Revelation 12:11). After the 1,000 years, the New Jerusalem city will come down out of heaven to this earth (see Revelation 21:1-3). Following the second resurrection, the wicked will surround the crystal clear walls (see Revelation 20:5-9). By God's amazing grace we hope to find ourselves on the right side of those walls, the inside.

But what about those on the outside? While they have chosen to be enemies of Christ, some of them may be former work partners, neighbors, acquaintances, friends, distant relatives, or even dearly loved ones and fellow church members. How will we then look upon those who may deserve our bitterest resentment? Will we think, "Now I'm finally going to let them have it? Before the wrath of God finishes them, I'm going to tell them what I *really* think of them." Will we point to them with self-righteous smugness and yell, "I told you so! You should have listened to me! You deserve what you're getting!" Will we laugh at them? Will any of the other saved saints laugh, mocking at the predicament of the lost with sarcastic delight? I don't think so. Having the mind of God, the character of our Redeemer, we will take "no pleasure in the death of him that dieth" (Ezekiel 18:32).

There will be only one attitude and one spirit pervading the ranks of the redeemed as their tear-filled faces look to the final destruction of the wicked. As their eyes meet the eyes of those they have reason to hate, the saints will only wish they might have known HOW they could have reached the sinful heart, what more they might have done. Yes, they give glory to God that sin's reign has finally ended; but they wish that they had done more to reach the lost. When it is too late, we may wish that we had engaged more committedly to enlarging God's kingdom.

Praise God, dear friends, it is not yet too late! We still have the chance to influence sinners for good. Keeping this picture ever before us, keeping God's grace ever upon us, we can love the sinner while hating sin with a perfect hatred. Yes, keeping the law of God is important, even the "conclusion of the whole matter," as Solomon says (see Eccleciastes 12:13), but only when we recognize that "all the law is fulfilled in one word, even in this: Thou shalt love thy neighbor as thyself" (Galatians 5:14).

With this self-sacrificing love of Jesus emanating from his entire being, Paul urged, "Let us not be weary in well doing: for in due season we shall reap, if we faint not. As we have therefore opportunity, let us *do good* unto all men, especially unto them who are of the household of faith" (Galatians 6:9, 10). *How?* By "considering thyself"— that it is the *"goodness and forbearance and longsuffering . . . of God"* that "leadeth thee to repentance" (Galatians 6:1; Romans 2:4).

Do you see, dear friend, that we can have that heart of love for the sinner while we maintain hatred for sin?

Oh, Father in heaven, please give us Your heart of love for all mankind, through the grace of our Lord Jesus Christ. May Christ be in us and may the mystery of godliness be in His remnant church. For Jesus' sake. *Amen.*